SCHOOLCRAFT COLLEGE LIBRARY

W9-AFS-942

HB
3730
.S47

Silk, Leonard
Primer on business
forecasting

WITHDRAWN

BRADNER LIBRARY
SCHOOLCRAFT COLLEGE
LIVONIA, MICHIGAN 48152

A Primer on
BUSINESS FORECASTING

A Primer on

The Primer series is under the editorial supervision of

PETER L. BERNSTEIN

BUSINESS FORECASTING

With a Guide to Sources of Business Data

Leonard S. Silk and
M. Louise Curley

 RANDOM HOUSE   *New York*

HB
3730
.S47

Copyright © 1970 by Random House, Inc.
All rights reserved under International and Pan-American Copyright
Conventions.
Published in the United States by Random House, Inc., New York, and
simultaneously in Canada by Random House of Canada Limited,
Toronto.
Library of Congress Catalog Card Number: 72–93528
Manufactured in the United States of America by Colonial Press, Inc.,
Clinton, Mass.

FIRST PRINTING

9 8 7 6 5 4 3 2

For Bernice and Tom

"Methinks I am a prophet new inspired. . . ."

SHAKESPEARE, *Richard II*

Contents

Introduction

If you go to Salzburg, your guide will point out to you the house where the town hangman once lived. It stands in an open field, far from the houses of the other good burghers. Salzburg needed its hangman but saw no reason for liking him.

The economic forecaster is in a somewhat similar position in the business world. He is disliked when his prophecies are ominous; he is distrusted when they are cheerful; and he is reviled when they turn out wrong. Nevertheless, the forecaster survives and even prospers because business decision makers feel that they need him. They know that business decisions are inherently future-oriented and risk-laden, and they want analyses of statistical data and other economic, political, and market information as a means of reducing the risks that they face.

Management decisions in the areas of investment, production, purchasing, finance, personnel, marketing, inventory building or cutting, and capital spending on new plants and equipment depend upon the answers to such questions as the following:

What will the general state of business be? What will be the demand for our products?

How much will materials cost? Will the materials we need

be available? What particular shortages or surpluses are likely to develop?

Will we be able to get the number and kinds of employees we will need? Or will we be laying off people? What is going to happen to wage rates?

What will be the effect on our sales if we change our prices? What are our competitors likely to do?

Where will the growing markets for our products be? What new industrial or regional developments are likely to create new opportunities for us? Should we be switching to different types of production? What types of new products ought we to be developing?

Have we enough production capacity to meet probable future demand?

Considering what is happening to costs and what we expect to happen to sales, what will our future financial position be?

What outside financing will we require? What is it likely to cost us? Is this a good time to seek it, or should we wait?

Should we be working down our inventories? Or are we likely to be caught short?

Questions like these go to the very heart of the managerial problem. The answers to all such questions necessitate forecasting. Thus, the problem for business management is not whether to forecast—it must—but how to forecast. Management must decide whether its forecasting will be done mainly by hunch and instinct, or whether forecasts will be prepared as intelligently as possible. Though hunch and instinct—and hope or fear—will always play their parts in business decisions, modern American management is turning more and more to forecasting methods which are systematic, thorough, and objective. While business forecasts cannot be expected to be as dependable and exact as predictions made in the physical sciences, business forecasts can be constructed in accordance with what is called "scientific method"—that is, attempting to collect all information relevant to the problem and drawing logical inferences from this information.

Business forecasting requires time and work and, for the best results, economic skills of a high order. Business has grown so big and complex that managements of many companies find themselves confronted by tasks where decisions based on hunch or old rules of thumb are liable to large and costly mistakes. Under these circumstances, management is increasingly turning to professional economists for forecasting and other business research. However, even if a company can afford to employ outstanding economic talent, high-level executives cannot delegate to staff economists or outside consultants the responsibility for making final judgments about the business outlook and what it implies for their particular business. Management, therefore, should seek always to improve its competence in this important field. Business economists and statisticians, on their side, need to view their research from the perspective of managerial decision makers and to make their conclusions as clear, firm, and policy-oriented as possible.

In this book, we have tried to avoid encouraging anyone to expect too much from forecasting. Business will always remain to some extent a gamble. But a good gambler constantly tries to get the best odds that he can. In business the odds must improve when management acts on the basis of full and up-to-date information and careful analysis of the changing business picture. In the chapters that follow we have tried to set down, as simply and succinctly as possible, the essential facts about this painful but important subject to guide students of business and economics, as well as businessmen.

The book is divided into three parts: Part One explains the principal techniques of business forecasting, which we have grouped as the deterministic, symptomatic, and systematic approaches; Part Two describes and evaluates the most important data; and Part Three provides an index of source materials for those readers who want to acquire data about a particular subject or to assemble a comprehensive working library of current economic information.

If you have a serious interest in learning how to forecast, you should—after a first reading of Parts One and Two—set yourself some real problem, such as forecasting general business activity in the next twelve months, the level of automobile sales or housing construction, or some other subject that concerns you. You should then go back to find those procedures in Part One that bear on your particular problem; you may want to consult some of the articles and books included in the selected bibliography at the end of Part One. You must then construct a simple forecasting plan or model, review Part Two for the data available to deal with your problem, and assemble the necessary information from the sources listed in Part Three. After you have produced your numerical forecast, you should periodically check it and revise it as new information becomes available.

Active involvement is the only way to learn forecasting (or perhaps anything else). It should produce humility, sympathy for the problems of other forecasters, and, we think, confidence that logical analysis of historical and current information can usually produce reasonable inferences about the future.

LEONARD S. SILK
M. LOUISE CURLEY

PART I

Methods of
Business Forecasting

CHAPTER 1

Strategies of Forecasting

Any logical approach to business forecasting is based on three assumptions:

1. that economic magnitudes—such as levels of production, income, prices, wages, interest rates, and consumer expenditures—are bound together in a system that has considerable stability over time;
2. that future changes in those magnitudes will result, to an appreciable extent, from presently operating causes, or may be deduced from presently observable symptoms;
3. that the nature of those symptoms or causes, and their probable future consequences, may be discovered by studying past experience.

From these assumptions—which underlie not only business forecasting but the whole of economic theory and statistics—three basic strategies of forecasting are derived: the deterministic, the symptomatic, and the systematic strategies. These may best be illustrated by analogies drawn from other fields.

The *deterministic* strategy assumes that the present has a close causal relation to the future. This is the strategy that would be used by a cardsharp, who had stacked the deck of cards, to predict the deal. In economic forecasting, the strategy would be used to predict construction expenditures by a knowledge of construction contract awards already made.

The *symptomatic* strategy assumes that present signs show

how the future is developing; such signs do not "determine" the future but reveal the process of change that is already taking place. Thus, a falling barometer may reveal a coming storm, or a rising body thermometer an incipient illness. In economic forecasting, this strategy calls for the spotting of "leading indicators"—time series whose movements foreshadow rises or declines in general business activity.

The *systematic* strategy assumes that, though changes in the real world may seem accidental or chaotic, careful analysis can reveal certain underlying regularities (sometimes called principles, theories, or laws). The way to find these regularities is to black out much of reality and hold only to the abstractions that make up a system, such as a solar system, or a nuclear system, or an economic system. Though the theories that result from this process of abstraction are "unreal," they may nevertheless possess the power to affect the real world—provided, of course, that the theories are sound. The test of the soundness of a theory is how it measures up when applied to reality: An atomic explosion confirms Einstein's $E = mc^2$. Similarly, a price cut that leads to increased sales confirms the hypothetical demand curve that no man has ever seen outside an economics textbook. To be sure, economic "laws" do not have the consistency of those in the physical sciences. Nevertheless, economic relations or theories, derived from a study of the past, may be useful tools for prediction, within some acceptable range of probable error.

In this book we have classified available forecasting techniques under the three above-mentioned strategies. Each of the three strategies has characteristics that will continue to make it an indispensable part of the business forecaster's tool kit.

The great advantage of the simplest approach to forecasting, the deterministic method, is its very simplicity. As the logical principle known as Occam's razor states, it is vain to do with more what can be done with less. So it would have been vain in a period of defense build-up, such as World War II, for a business economist to have performed vast and complex analyses to predict the government's steel or copper requirements—assuming he could examine the official document governing procurement requirements. Because of its emphasis upon the necessity of full, fast, and accurate reporting as part of the forecasting operation, and because, under many circumstances, it is the surest forecasting technique, the deterministic approach will never be made obsolete by more "sophisticated" methods.

Nevertheless, the accuracy of forecasts produced by the deterministic method varies greatly—and it varies inversely with the length of time to be covered by the forecast. While today's plans may not be changed tomorrow, they may be changed next month, and will almost certainly be changed next year. Thus, it is no violation of Occam's principle to suggest that it may be necessary—for instance, in forecasting capital spending by business—to supplement the findings of capital spending surveys by economic analyses that try to weigh the effect of expected changes in general business activity upon announced capital spending plans. In such a case, the simplest and most direct solution to the forecasting problem may be inadequate. To deal with any extremely complicated forecasting problem —such as the course of the American economy for a year or more ahead—it is obvious that there can be no deterministic solution. Even Soviet economists cannot perfectly predict their nation's economic development far into the future just from the official Five-Year plan. Social, economic, or political realities may spoil the plan.

The particular advantage of the symptomatic or leading indicator approach is its concentration upon one of the most important problems for the business forecaster in a free economy: the determination of a coming turning point in the business cycle. Some analysts prefer to consider the implications of a large number of indicators separately, without attempting to blend them into a combined index; others find it useful to synthesize a forecasting index out of the separate time series. But few, if any, analysts would put their trust solely in the movements of the leading indicators, whether taken singly or combined. The great majority of analysts would regard forecasting by the indicators alone as too mechanistic, and would seek further explanations of the probable future course of business through general economic analysis of the underlying forces affecting business.

The systematic approach to business forecasting is essential for the diagnosis of complex problems in which the interaction of many factors must be analyzed. The forecaster using this approach may carefully define his assumptions and set up his analysis in strict mathematical formulas, derived from his measurement of past relationships of economic factors; this is the so-called econometric or model-building approach. Or the forecaster, though taking an essentially systematic approach, may prefer to deal with the available data less rigorously and to depend more upon his intuitions and common sense.

The great advantage of the less rigorous approach is that it enables the analyst to range freely over the whole terrain of factors that relate to his problem and to employ his insights in reaching conclusions that could not be rigorously derived from the evidence but which, nevertheless, may prove more nearly correct than the results of "correct" logic. Some economists feel that the trouble with the econometric approach is that it assumes a consistency of relationships among economic variables that is not supported by the facts of the real world.

Still, the strict, econometric approach has many advantages: It prevents the economist from "faking"—that is, pretending to have worked out an analysis of many factors when he has only stated what the factors are and has produced a conclusion that has slight, if any, relationship to the factors discussed; it takes full advantage of the evidence of past economic relations and events, and does this in a way that can be checked; it clearly discards obsolete or erroneous theories; and it can be usefully applied to many intricate business problems, such as the demand for particular products or future movements of costs. (But one should bear in mind that in many instances—such as the market for a new and untried product —the best way to forecast demand might be a market research study.) For many business analysts, even a simple econometric model can be a useful start in the preparation of a forecast; it may give the first approximation of the forecast's structure, on which the analyst can continue to build.

From the preceding discussion, it becomes apparent that the approach taken in this book toward available forecasting techniques is eclectic. In some fields, such an approach might simply be a slipshod way of avoiding the task of making firm critical judgments, rather than discarding methods that are inferior or redundant. But, in business forecasting, an approach that tries to take advantage of the best qualities of several techniques is necessary for three reasons:

1. The wide variety of types of forecasting problems calls for the use of quite different techniques.
2. The record of no single forecasting technique has been so unerring as to eliminate all other methods.
3. In a field where no technique can be depended upon always to yield accurate results, it is desirable to check the forecasts obtained by one method against those reached by other methods.

CHAPTER 2

Deterministic Techniques of Forecasting

Deterministic techniques are used where a close causal connection or a rough identity is perceived between present and future. The term "deterministic," however, is not meant to imply an absolutely fixed and irreversible relation between present and future. In the real economic world, completely fixed relationships do not exist. Deterministic techniques may be used either to forecast particular elements, such as capital spending, residential construction, or consumer expenditures, or, often in combination with other methods, to forecast general business conditions. The principal deterministic techniques are discussed in the following pages.

Latest Information

This technique, which is of great importance for short-run forecasting, is built on the assumption that economic magnitudes and relationships change slowly. Hence, with the latest information, one can generally assume that existing conditions or trends will continue for some time into the future. For instance, one can make a reasonably good record as a weather forecaster by always saying that tomorrow's weather will be the same as today's. Similarly, one can do very well as a business forecaster (assuming that the short run is the only concern) by always predicting that next week's business will be the same as this week's, or that the current trend of business will last for a time. This way only the turning points are missing.

This technique is obviously naive—but that does not make it any less important to business for dealing with such problems as setting weekly or even monthly production schedules, ordering merchandise, setting prices, and the like.

However complicated or sophisticated the forecasting operation may become, a business can never dispense with the necessity for fast reporting and analysis of all the significant facts about the changing business picture. Although the forecasting "principle" involved is simple or naive, the task of collecting, digesting, and evaluating the latest information can be as difficult as anyone could demand.

Published statistics may be anywhere from a day to several months late. Pieces of information—whether reported in the newspapers and magazines, in the market place, or in the board room—may be true, partially true, or false. Many kinds of information, essential to the appraisal of a business problem (such as decisions by other businessmen or by government officials), may be concealed or revealed in a distorted form for tactical or political reasons. Much information may be colored by the spokesman's concern with "public relations" or by his unconscious, wishful thinking. Even an accurate report may be suspect; the fact that a decision is known may cause it to be changed. Data may be so voluminous as to be out of date before they can be collated and analyzed. The contribution of fast and accurate reporting to business forecasting cannot be overestimated.

Knowledge of Programs or Limits

A number of important factors bearing on the economic future are determined in advance and can be expected to remain virtually stable, or to change at a foreseeable rate, through the forecast period—such as budgeted government expenditures on goods and services, statutory tax provisions, capital budgets of business corporations, business contracts, population and labor force, wage rates determined by collective bargaining contracts or by minimum wage legislation, industrial capacity, the stock of houses or automobiles of some specified age. These factors may be important in and of themselves, and they may also be used as elements that will affect, but not be significantly affected by, economic developments during the forecast period. They may be the limiting factors on other, more variable types of economic activity. For example, a forecast of the production of consumer durable goods during a war emergency would depend essentially upon the availability of steel for civilian use, after essential military programs had taken their share of the steel industry's total-capacity output. (It is assumed that the general situation during the defense build-up will be one of full employment and high consumer demand.)

Spotting the Beginning of a Lengthy Process

Certain immediate facts can be regarded either as causes or early phases of future economic activities. Many such facts are available to the businessman. Contracts for residential and industrial building, for instance, precede actual construction; the shipping of coal and iron ore precedes steel production;

new orders or unfilled orders of manufacturers largely determine production; mortgage and installment debt contracted by consumers largely determine future repayments; approved company plans for investment in plant and equipment precede the execution of those plans.

In none of these cases is there a perfect causal connection between the initial and later stages of the process. Construction work may be delayed or accelerated; contracts may be cancelled; new orders may represent duplicate ordering for fear of shortages or strikes; floods, material or manpower shortages may curtail production; consumers may default on debts or change their "propensities" to spend or save; businesses may delay or cancel capital spending and expansion plans. Nevertheless, a close enough relation between the initial and later stages of an economic process will usually exist to make forecasting on the basis of advance information feasible.

Diagnosing People's Expectations

The so-called expectational or psychological approach assumes that the states of mind of businessmen and consumers play a determining role in economic developments and that surveys of their expectations will have forecasting value. Many economists, however, believe that the causal sequence between expectations and objective economic conditions runs just the reverse of the way the psychological approach assumes. Thus, expectations are more a result of objective business conditions than a cause of those conditions.

We find it difficult to make a hard-and-fast conclusion about this. In particular circumstances—as, say, the blow to investor confidence of President Eisenhower's heart attack in 1955, which produced a sharp break in the market—it is obvious that states of mind and expectations actually had real economic consequences. But in other circumstances, expectations seem to follow real developments—as in periods when public optimism has apparently reached its peak at the end of a boom.

At minimum, it is safe to say that business observers should be curious about public states of mind and expectations, which often derive from a detailed knowledge of individuals' judgments of their own "objective conditions," their financial status, employment prospects, and the like. In an economy like ours, the decisions of private individuals, as producers or consumers, cannot be predicted wholly on the basis of economic data; hence, attempts to discover significant changes in public optimism or pessimism, which may imply greater or lesser willingness to spend or invest, may reveal information that an economist should attempt to relate to a broader analysis based upon more objective economic and financial information.

Some of the principal surveys of business or consumer expectations are:

McGraw-Hill Department of Economics surveys of capital spending plans

Securities and Exchange Commission–U.S. Department of Commerce surveys of capital spending plans

National Industrial Conference Board–*Newsweek* surveys of capital appropriations

Survey Research Center of the University of Michigan consumer surveys

U.S. Department of Commerce, Bureau of Census consumer surveys

Dun & Bradstreet surveys of businessmen's expectations

Monthly business survey of the National Association of Purchasing Agents

Railroad shippers' forecasts, conducted under auspices of the American Association of Railroads

Fortune surveys, including surveys of business expectations and mood, retail sales, farm spending, homebuilding, inventories, and capital goods production

Manufacturers' sales and inventory expectations of the U.S. Department of Commerce

Expectational surveys of this type are a broader application of one of the traditional business approaches to the forecasting problem: asking one's salesmen or dealers how much they expect to sell in a coming period.

The most serious weaknesses in such polls or surveys is that people may not know their own minds, may not plan very far ahead, may not be able to perceive the circumstances that will cause them to change their intentions, or may inaccurately report their intentions or expectations for various reasons. For instance, a salesman may seek to avoid committing himself to selling too large a quota; a consumer may seek to impress the interviewer. Nevertheless, expectational surveys may be the best way of catching a big switch in public attitudes which statistical evidence alone cannot explain. Surveys of consumer intentions to buy certain durable goods, such as automobiles, have shown a fair degree of reliability, and they have been useful as a basis for studies of consumer decision making.

An important development in the collection of data on consumer buying intentions is the attempt to measure buying expectations in terms of subjective probabilities of the purchaser. Largely under the impetus of work pioneered by F. Thomas Juster,[1] the U.S. Bureau of the Census has adopted a new technique to make such a measurement. From an answer sheet scaled from 0 to 100, each respondent selects his chance of purchasing given items and his chances of experiencing a substantial change in his income. The results are then shown in terms of mean probabilities, that is, the average values reported by respondents as to their chances of purchasing an item or expecting a change in income. The Commercial Credit Company has gone a step further by

[1] F. Thomas Juster, *Anticipations and Purchases: An Analysis of Consumer Behavior* (Princeton, N.J.: Princeton University Press, 1964).

taking the basic data of the Bureau of the Census and developing projections of consumer demand for selected household appliances and automobiles in units and dollar totals. These projections are published quarterly in *Consumer Buying Prospects.*

Surveys of business spending plans can be expected to have a much greater degree of firmness than those of individual persons. Capital expenditure surveys, such as those of McGraw-Hill's Department of Economics and the Securities and Exchange Commission–Department of Commerce, are among the forecaster's most valuable tools. Yet these capital spending surveys cannot be taken as solid proof of future business outlays on plant and equipment. Businesses often alter their rates of expenditure, despite earlier plans, according to changes in the business cycle. The analyst must adjust the findings of the capital spending surveys for his general conclusions about upswings or downswings in the business cycle. In upswings, capital spending usually runs ahead of earlier plans; in downswings, it lags behind.

CHAPTER 3

Symptomatic Techniques
of Forecasting

The symptomatic approach to forecasting is based on the concept that, though the business cycle represents a highly complicated set of relationships among different economic variables, the general sequence of events in a business cycle is sufficiently consistent to enable an analyst to forecast coming changes by watching the "leading indicators." The importance of the symptomatic approach to the business observer is its concentration upon the task of spotting turning points in business activity.

For many years business analysts have been searching for a single indicator, or set of indicators for these turning points, which would always lead general business developments. Some thought they had found such indicators in stock market activity, interest rates, pig iron production, carloadings, Dun & Bradstreet's index of business failures, and so forth. The debate over which of these are "old wives' indicators" and which possess real leading characteristics continues today.

Indicators of the National Bureau of Economic Research

The National Bureau of Economic Research (NBER) has been conducting detailed statistical analyses of business cycles for more than three decades and has done an exhaustive job of screening time series with forecasting value.

Before World War II, Wesley C. Mitchell and Arthur F. Burns, after analyzing approximately 500 monthly or quarterly series, selected 70 that regularly traced the business cycle, of which 21 indicators were judged to be the most trustworthy.[1] After the war, it seemed advisable for the bureau to screen all the series again—both because later information was available and because political and economic changes might have rendered the Mitchell-Burns studies obsolete. The task of bringing their work up-to-date was undertaken by Geoffrey H. Moore, who published the results of his findings in 1950.[2] Moore started with a collection of 801 series, of which he found 255 to be acceptable indicators, and 21 most reliable. Moore concluded that:

1. Cyclical turning points of different series are rather widely dispersed in business cycles. While peaks and troughs in each of 400 series, selected for the regularity of their behavior, tended to cluster around peaks and troughs in aggregate economic activity, each cluster was spread over one to three years.

2. A group of series can be selected whose turning points typically precede cyclical turns in business activity; another group can be selected whose turns roughly coincide with aggregate turns; and a third group can be selected whose turns characteristically lag behind turns in aggregate activity.

3. Series in all three timing groups are useful in anticipating and identifying cyclical revivals and recessions. The series

[1] *Statistical Indicators of Cyclical Revivals*, Bulletin 69 (New York: National Bureau of Economic Research, May 1938). Reprinted in Geoffrey H. Moore (ed.), *Business Cycle Indicators*, 1 (Princeton, N.J.: Princeton University Press for National Bureau of Economic Research, 1961), 162–183.
[2] *Statistical Indicators of Cyclical Revivals and Recessions*, Occasional Paper No. 31 (New York: National Bureau of Economic Research, 1950). Reprinted in Moore, *Business Cycle Indicators*, Vol. 1, pp. 184–260.

collectively can be particularly helpful in facilitating prompt recognition of a development once it occurs.

Nevertheless, Moore's study suggested that interpretation of the indicators would be subject to numerous difficulties and uncertainties—the chief ones being (1) to determine whether a change in a particular series, at the time it occurs, is only a temporary dip or rise or really represents a reversal of trend; (2) to relate the significance of the changes in each series to the others—since virtually all of the series are to some extent variable and erratic; and (3) to get the data for each series on a current basis.

As Gerhard Colm pointed out, Moore's leading series are of three general sorts: (1) "deterministic" series, such as new orders, residential building contracts, and commercial building contracts; (2) speculative or anticipatory series, such as the stock market index and the wholesale price index of basic commodities; and (3) sensitive measures of current change, such as business failures, new incorporations, and the average work week.[3] Each series in the leading group reaches its turning point from two to ten months before turns in the business cycle; each series in the lagging group follows turns in the business cycle by two to seven months. The variability of lead and lag times is obviously a hazard for the forecaster; allowing for the time until the data are actually received, the indicators may on occasion give little or no lead time.

Work on the leading indicator approach to forecasting has been facilitated by the computer. In 1957 the U.S. Bureau of the Census, at the request of Raymond J. Saulnier, then chairman of the Council of Economic Advisers, started a research program to develop a monthly report on statistical indicators. The list of leading, coincident, and lagging indicators was to be selected by the National Bureau of Economic Research. Using the newly developed techniques of seasonal

[3] Gerhard Colm, "Economic Barometers and Economic Models," *Review of Economics and Statistics,* 37 (February 1955), 57.

adjustment, the Bureau of the Census began publication of its report *Business Cycle Developments* (now called *Business Conditions Digest*) in October 1961. The first edition contained an updated version of the indicator list that was published by NBER in 1960; its short list of indicators was comprised of twelve leading indicators, nine coincident, and five lagging.

The most recent revision of the statistical indicators took place in 1966.[4] The short list now includes twenty-five series, of which twelve are leading, seven coincident, and six lagging. In addition to updating the list, several new techniques have been introduced. First, the selected list of indicators has been classified by economic process as well as by timing to facilitate more analysis. The economic processes identified are shown in Table 1, together with the number of leading, coincident, and lagging indicators in each process. Thus, under fixed cap-

Table 1 *The National Bureau's Economic Indicators*

Economic Process	Number of Indicators		
	Leading	Coincident	Lagging
Employment and unemployment	2	2	1
Production, income, consumption, and trade		5	
Fixed capital investment	4		1
Inventories and inventory investment	1		1
Prices, costs, and profits	4		1
Money and credit	1		2

ital investment, for example, new investment commitments, such as new orders, are leading indicators and investment expenditures on new plant and equipment are lagging indicators.

Another innovation in the leading indicator approach is an explicit scoring plan to aid the selection and evaluation

---

[4] Geoffrey H. Moore and Julius Shiskin, *Indicators of Business Expansions and Contractions*, Occasional Paper No. 103 (New York: Columbia University Press for National Bureau of Economic Research, 1967).

of indicators. Six criteria for selection have been set up: economic significance; statistical adequacy; historical conformity to business cycles; cyclical timing record; smoothness; and promptness of publication. Each series is assigned a score within a range from 0 to 100. While, admittedly, the scoring is subjective on the part of the authors, it does help the subsequent user in formulating his own judgment. Table 2 shows the 1966 short list together with scores for the six criteria and other relevant information.

Diffusion Indexes

To deal with one of the chief difficulties of interpreting the individual indicators—the problem of knowing whether change in any particular series is really forecasting a reversal in the general trend or is an isolated development—Geoffrey Moore devised what he called the diffusion index. This is based on his finding that business cycle movements "have invariably been preceded by a remarkably regular cycle in the proportion of industrial activities undergoing expansion or contraction," and that with economic time series as with human beings, "the individual is more variable than the group."[5]

To make his diffusion index, Moore first smoothed the individual series by means of moving averages, using longer moving averages for the more erratic series; he then combined the series in each of the leading, coincident, and lagging groups by counting the number of series in each group that are rising at a given time. He converted that number into a percentage of the number of indicators in the group. Thus, when the percentage was below 50, more indicators were con-

---

[5] Geoffrey H. Moore, "Analyzing Business Cycles," *American Statistician*, 9 (April–May 1954), 13.

Table 2 Short List of Indicators: Scores and Timing Characteristics

Classification and Series Title (1)	First Business Cycle Turn Covered (2)	Scores, Six Criteria							Timing at Peaks and Troughs				
		Average Score (3)	Economic Significance (4)	Statistical Adequacy (5)	Conformity (6)	Timing (7)	Smoothness (8)	Currency (9)	Business Cycle Turns Covered (10)	Leads (11)	Rough Coincidences* (12)	Lags (13)	Median Lead(−) or Lag(+) in Months (14)
Leading indicators (12 series)													
1. Average work week, production workers, manufacturing	1921	66	50	65	81	66	60	80	19	13	4(2)	2	−5
30. Nonagricultural placements, BES	1945	68	75	63	63	58	80	80	10	8	4(0)	1	−3
38. Index of net business formation	1945	68	75	58	81	67	80	40	10	8	3(1)	0	−7
6. New orders, durable goods industries	1920	78	75	72	88	84	60	80	20	16	7(1)	0	−4
10. Contracts and orders, plant and equipment	1948	64	75	63	92	50	40	40	8	7	2(0)	1	−6
29. New building permits, private housing units	1918	67	50	60	76	80	60	80	22	17	5(1)	1	−6
31. Change in book value, manufacturing and trade inventories	1945	65	75	67	77	78	20	40	10	9	2(1)	0	−8
23. Industrial materials prices	1919	67	50	72	79	44	80	100	21	13	9(4)	2	−2
19. Stock prices, 500 common stocks	1873	81	75	74	77	87	80	100	44	33	14(2)	5	−4
16. Corporate profits after taxes, quarterly	1920	68	75	70	79	76	60	25	20	13	11(4)	2	−2
17. Ratio, price to unit labor cost, manufacturing	1919	69	50	67	84	72	60	80	21	17	10(1)	3	−3
113. Change in consumer installment debt	1929	63	50	79	77	60	60	40	14	11	4(0)	1	−10

Roughly coincident indicators (7 series)

41. Employees in nonagricultural establishments	1929	81	75	61	90	87	100	80	14	6	12(6)	2	0
43. Unemployment rate, total (inverted)	1929	75	75	63	96	60	80	80	14	4	8(3)	6	0
50. GNP in constant dollars, quarterly expenditure estimate, quarterly	1921	73	75	75	91	58	80	50	17	7	9(3)	3	−2
47. Industrial production	1919	72	75	63	94	38	100	80	21	9	13(9)	3	0
52. Personal income	1921	74	75	73	89	43	100	80	19	10	12(2)	5	−1
816. Manufacturing and trade sales	1948	71	75	68	70	80	80	40	8	4	6(4)	0	0
54. Sales of retail stores	1919	69	75	77	89	12	80	100	21	5	7(1)	6	0

Lagging indicators (6 series)

502. Unemployment rate, persons unemployed 15+ weeks (inverted)	1948	69	50	63	98	52	80	80	8	1	5(1)	6	+2
61. Business expenditures, plant and equipment, quarterly	1918	86	75	77	96	94	100	80	20	2	16(5)	13	+1
71. Book value, manufacturing and trade inventories	1945	71	75	67	75	66	100	40	10	2	7(0)	8	+2
62. Labor cost per unit of output, manufacturing	1919	68	50	70	83	56	80	80	21	0	1(0)	14	+8
72. Commercial and industrial loans outstanding	1937	57	50	47	67	20	100	100	12	1	6(0)	7	+2
67. Bank rates, short-term business loans, quarterly	1919	60	50	55	82	47	80	50	21	2	5(1)	15	+5

* Rough coincidences include exact coincidences (shown in parentheses) and leads and lags of three months or less. Leads (lags) include leads (lags) of one month or more. The total number of timing comparisons, which can be less than the number of business cycle turns covered by the series, is the sum of the leads, exact coincidences, and lags. Leads and lags of quarterly series are expressed in terms of months.

Source: Geoffrey H. Moore and Julius Shiskin, *Indicators of Business Expansions and Contractions,* Occasional Paper No. 103 (New York: Columbia University Press for National Bureau of Economic Research, 1967), p. 68.

tracting than expanding; when it was above 50, more were expanding than contracting.

Such diffusion indexes must be used with care. From 1946 to 1951, as Moore notes, the leading curve dropped below the 50 percent line four times (mid-1946, early 1947, late 1947, early 1951) when no generally recognized business recession followed. In those instances, the roughly coincident curve showed corresponding movements. But, notes Moore, "The lagging curve did not participate in these 'abortive recessions.' Only in 1948 to 1949 did all three curves drop substantially below 50 per cent and remain there for several months."[6] The indicators were also misleading in 1956 and 1962. One must be wary of false signals being given off by the leading indicators. They may be flashing only a slowdown in the rate of expansion or a lull rather than an actual downturn in the business cycle.

Moore's conclusion is that, to distinguish the genuine from the abortive recession or revival, all three diffusion curves must be looked at, not just one. A further test of whether a swing in the curves is signaling a change in general business is how much the curves rise or fall and how long they remain at an extreme level. Moore concedes that these diffusion indexes are simply "mechanical summaries" of the economic data on which they are based. He insists that the curves be regarded as aids to, not substitutes for, careful study and analysis of the underlying data.

Not all economists think the diffusion index is a significant step forward. Arthur L. Broida, for instance, holds that the "remarkably regular cycle" of the historical measures is derived "by separating cyclical turning points from all other changes in direction sometime after the event with the omniscience of hindsight."[7] He suggests that hindsight is needed in

---

[6] *Ibid.*, p. 16.
[7] Arthur L. Broida, "Diffusion Indexes," *American Statistician,* 9 (June 1955), 16.

order to identify the cyclical turning points in the individual series, since at the time the turn occurs, it is not certain whether the turn represents only a wiggle or is real. In addition, all the indicators are highly variable. Hence, Broida concludes that the diffusion curves, though impressive as forecasters historically, cannot be of much current help without the detailed knowledge of the future that would make them unnecessary.

Current diffusion indexes appear to signify only what statisticians have long observed—that a slower rate of increase or decrease in any time series generally precedes a reversal of its direction. However, Broida does concede that, because of the general resemblance between diffusion indexes and rates of change, the diffusion measures may be useful for interpolating between aggregate values available at infrequent intervals or for approximating movements in an aggregate that is currently unavailable. Broida also insists that it is important to go behind the indicators, to discover why they are behaving as they are, rather than to use them mechanically. But Moore and many others who pay attention to leading indicators and diffusion indexes would agree with this position.

If regarded only as a simple and preliminary technique for relating the behavior of several different sorts of data to get a quick, current picture of the economic trend, the diffusion index can be a useful device. When a diffusion index is dropping, it may be regarded as a blinking yellow light, signaling caution to the analyst. In a field so rife with uncertainties, such cautionary signals are not to be despised or ignored.

Although the diffusion index provides a simple method of handling the problem of the variability of individual series, it is less helpful as a solution to the problems of spotting the turning points of individual time series, of indicating just how far ahead a turning point in the business cycle may be, or how steep a drop or how sharp a rise is in the offing. In general, the diffusion index of leading series precedes the business cycle turns by about six months, and the amplitude and speed of its movement correlate roughly with the nearness and probable intensity of a change in general business activity. In practice, however, any careful economist should treat the diffusion indexes—and each of the separate time series—with great caution, and should hesitate to date future cycle turns closely on this basis alone.

Amplitude-adjusted Indexes

A more sophisticated approach to the problem of combining the individual indicators into composite indexes has been developed by Julius Shiskin.[8] These indexes are called amplitude-adjusted composite indexes and are constructed by standardizing the month-to-month percentage changes of each series so that all series are expressed in comparable units. Each series is adjusted so that its average month-to-month change, without regard to direction, is equal to 1. If a series shows a value of 2 this means it is rising twice as fast as its average rate of change in the past. Each standardized series is then weighted according to the scores described earlier in the discussion of the new 1966 NBER list and combined into an index. The index is then also standardized. A further refinement adjusts the leading index to make its long-run trend the same as that of the index of the coincident series. This adjustment improves the cyclical comparability among the leading, coincident, and lagging indexes by removing most of the differences in long-run trend.[9] Amplitude-adjusted indexes of the leading, coin-

[8] Julius Shiskin, "Appendix A," *Signals of Recession and Recovery*, Occasional Paper No. 77 (New York: National Bureau of Economic Research, 1961), pp. 123–141.
[9] For a detailed description of the trend adjustment, see Julius Shiskin, "Reverse Trend Adjustment of Leading Indicators," *Review of Economics and Statistics*, 49 (February 1967), 45–49.

cident, and lagging indicators are currently published in *Business Conditions Digest,* the successor to the original *Business Cycle Developments.*

Like diffusion indexes, amplitude-adjusted indexes of the leading indicators tend to precede business-cycle turns by about six months. It is possible to relate changes in the amplitude-adjusted index to subsequent changes in specific measures of aggregate economic activity such as gross national product (GNP) and industrial production. Both Moore and Shiskin have worked out these relationships and have used them to predict GNP. They both, however, would admit that this technique should be used primarily as a check on the results of other more analytical approaches. Moore has said:

> It is not a substitute for a carefully reasoned approach to the economic outlook, whether this approach takes the shape of an econometric model or of a less formal apparatus. All I would claim is that the method helps to summarize the information contained in a group of leading indicators regarding the near-term future course of GNP or other variables that are systematically related to the business cycle. Hence it can provide the forecaster with some of the information useful in developing his actual forecast, and it can be used as a standard by which to judge his past efforts, perhaps helping him to improve upon them.[10]

Leading Monetary Indicators

The leading monetary indicator approach to forecasting is a special case of the symptomatic technique. Whereas the leading indicator approach is supported by the concept that the general sequence of events in a business cycle is sufficiently

---

[10] Geoffrey H. Moore, "Forecasting Short-Term Economic Change," *Journal of the American Statistical Association,* 64 (March 1969), 19.

Table 3 Lead of Monetary* Growth-Rate Turning Points Before Business-Cycle Turning Points

	Lead Before Downturns					Lead Before Upturns				
	Monetary Growth Rate Peaks†	Business Cycle Peaks†	Months Lead Series I	II	III	Monetary Growth Rate Troughs†	Business Cycle Troughs†	Months Lead Series I	II	III
Series I	Dec. 1918	Jan. 1920	13			Jan. 1921	July 1921	6		
Series II	Dec. 1918			13		June 1921			1	
Series III	Oct. 1919					Sept. 1921				−2
Series I	Dec. 1922	May 1923	5			Mar. 1923	July 1924	16		
Series II	June 1922			11		July 1923			12	
Series III	Jan. 1923				3	Feb. 1924				5
Series I	Aug. 1925	Oct. 1926	14			Dec. 1926	Nov. 1927	11		
Series II	Nov. 1924			23		Dec. 1926			11	
Series III	Feb. 1925				4	Dec. 1926				11
Series I	Jan. 1928	June 1929	17			Oct. 1931	Mar. 1933	7		
Series II	Oct. 1927			20		Mar. 1932			12	
Series III	Apr. 1928				20	July 1932				8
Series I	Aug. 1935	May 1937	21			Oct. 1937	June 1938	8		
Series II	June 1935			23		Dec. 1937			6	
Series III	Aug. 1935				14	Dec. 1937				6

Series	Monetary turn	Business turn	Lead (months)
Series I	Oct. 1951	July 1953	21
Series II	Nov. 1951		20
Series III	June 1952		13
Series I	July 1954	July 1957	36
Series II	Feb. 1955		29
Series III	Apr. 1955		27
Series I	July 1958	(?)	
Series II	July 1958		
Series III	Mar. 1959		
			147 162 120
	Range		5–36 11–29 3–27
	Average		18.1 19.9 14.6

Series	Monetary turn	Business turn	Lead (months)
Series I	Dec. 1948	Oct. 1949	10
Series II	June 1948		16
Series III	Feb. 1949		8
Series I	Nov. 1953	Aug. 1954	9
Series II	Nov. 1953		9
Series III	Apr. 1954		4
Series I	Aug. 1957	Apr. 1958	8
Series II	Jan. 1958		3
Series III	Jan. 1958		3
			85 69 43
	Range		5–17 1–16 −2 to 11
	Average		10.6 8.6 5.4

* Money supply = demand deposits adjusted plus currency, seasonally adjusted.

† Definition of growth rate series: Series I = computed as the percent change from the preceding month; Series II = computed as the six-month moving average of the percentage change from the preceding month plotted on the sixth month; Series III = computed as the percent change from the year-ago data.

‡ National Bureau of Economic Research datings are used.

Source: Beryl W. Sprinkel, "Monetary Growth as a Cyclical Predictor," *Journal of Finance*, 14 (September 1959), 338.

consistent to permit forecasts based on a group of leading indicators, the leading monetary indicator approach is based on the theory that the rate of growth in the money supply influences cyclical changes in business activity in a predictable manner and is, therefore, the most important factor in determining the future course of business. At present, the theory behind the monetary indicator approach is a subject of controversy. The leading theoretician of the monetary school of economics is Milton Friedman of the University of Chicago. Friedman is less interested in the problem of forecasting than in the policy implications of his theory, but some of his disciples have stressed the forecasting ability of monetary theory. For example, Beryl W. Sprinkel, economist for the Harris Trust and Savings Bank of Chicago, uses the growth of money supply as an important factor in his economic forecasts.[11] Sprinkel has plotted variants of the rate of growth of the money supply from 1909–1958 on a time chart showing recessions (as defined by the National Bureau of Economic Research). His results are summarized in Table 3. He found that recessions were preceded by reductions in the rate of growth of money supply and that recoveries were preceded by rises.

Sprinkel claims that the main determinant of the rate of growth of the money supply is Federal Reserve monetary policy. A move toward tightness by these monetary authorities will reduce the reserves available for lending or investing and will inhibit monetary growth. But in 1959, Sprinkel noted several caveats that should be made before using this approach mechanically. He concluded that:

> The leading monetary indicator approach to forecasting changes in the business trend promises to be a valuable *addition* to the kit of tools available to the economic forecaster. In assessing the value of this tool, results should be compared not only with perfection but also with the alternatives avail-

[11] Beryl W. Sprinkel, "Monetary Growth as a Cyclical Predictor," *Journal of Finance,* 14 (September 1959), 333–336.

able. Clearly, this technique does not eliminate all doubt about future business trends, but it does tend to reduce the range of uncertainty.[12]

The monetarist approach to economic analysis and forecasting poses a challenge to the dominant trend of central bank thinking, which maintains that interest rates are the controlling monetary factor for near-term spending—particularly investment outlays. The monetarists, following Friedman, stress that it is the quantity of money (however defined[13]) that controls spending.

The professionals are still uncertain as to which approach is more nearly correct. Many economists, however, are looking more sympathetically at Friedman's quantity theory approach than they were a few years ago. Paul A. Samuelson, for instance, says that where he would once have given one and a half cheers for the money supply as the critical variable influencing spending, he is now prepared to give two cheers. And, after examining some empirical evidence about the impact of interest rates versus the money supply on spending, Harry Johnson observes that "empirical researchers have had very mixed luck in verifying the hypothesized influence of interest rates on investment, let alone consumption expenditure, whereas Friedman and [David] Meiselman have had remarkable success in predicting changes in consumption expenditures, in both nominal and real terms, from changes in the money supply."[14] Yet, the majority of economists still feel that more research and testing is required before the monetarist

[12] *Ibid.*, p. 345. For the business analyst who is interested in the leading monetary indicator approach to forecasting, the Federal Reserve Bank of St. Louis, Missouri, in its *Monthly Review* and weekly and monthly publications on monetary trends and data is a valuable source of information. In fact, the St. Louis Federal Reserve Bank is considered a center of Friedman's economic disciples.

[13] See pp. 113–114.

[14] Harry G. Johnson, "Current Issues in Monetary Policy" (Paper presented at the Fifteenth Annual Monetary Conference of the American Bankers Association, Dorado Beach, Puerto Rico, May 24, 1968).

theory of forecasting can be completely accepted. There is need for more thorough investigation of the interest elasticity of the demand for money, the stability of the velocity or turn-over of money, the exact definition of money, and the time lags over which monetary policy affects the economy. "With all these real and interesting issues awaiting better answers than we now have," Wilfred Lewis, Jr. says, "it is rather unfortunate to have to waste time unraveling some of the more extreme pronouncements of the 'money is everything' school which have to do with semantics rather than the functioning of the economy."[15]

Miscellaneous Indicator Approaches

Many business analysts have their own favorite statistical indicators for forecasting either general business activity or movements in certain other time series. For example, Leonard Ayres of the Cleveland Trust Company had a high regard for bond price differentials—that is, the spread between low- and high-grade bonds—as a measure of business confidence. The rationale behind this index is that the price of high-grade issues principally reflects interest rates, while the price of more speculative issues reflects investors' attitudes toward risk factors; hence, the differential represents an evaluation of the risk premium over the nearly "pure" interest rate.

The stock market is, of course, a similar type of forecaster—though, obviously, not a wholly reliable one since investors and speculators can hardly be expected to always have clear foresight. In addition, outside factors, such as tax or credit

---

[15] Wilfred Lewis, Jr., " 'Money Is Everything' Economics—A Tempest in a Teapot," *The Record*, 6 (New York: National Industrial Conference Board, April 1969), 32.

measures and margin requirements, may exert influences that distort the purely expectational evidence of stock market movements.

The Federal Reserve Board's Consultant Committee on General Business Expectations has suggested a number of additional leading series that it considers useful for forecasting cyclical changes,[16] including the spread between high- and low-grade bonds, unfilled orders, forward investment commitments, other contracts, budgeted expenditures, other price indexes, employee accessions in manufacturing establishments,[17] and money turnover.

Statistical indicators have many advantages over other types of information for business analysts. They are relatively objective and accurate, cover all areas of the economy, are more or less historically comparable for their behavior in different business cycles (and thus their reliability can be more adequately tested), and are inexpensive (from the standpoint of the business user). They may also constitute the very factors causing the changing expectations of businessmen and consumers, which psychological surveys are attempting to measure. But the statistical indicators may avoid certain difficulties that are involved in the expectational or "mood" surveys, such as the fact that respondents' answers "may be provided carelessly, by uninformed persons, and possibly somewhat inarticulately,"[18] or that direct surveys, by necessity, cover a relatively small sample of respondents.

Time series data have the further advantage of being readily handled for forecasting purposes by modern statistical methods, such as the fitting and extrapolation of straight line or

---

[16] *Report of Consultant Committee on General Business Expectations* (Washington, D.C.: Board of Governors of Federal Reserve System, 1955), pp. 119–142.

[17] See also Geoffrey H. Moore, "Business Cycles and the Labor Market," *Monthly Labor Review*, 78 (March 1955), 288–292.

[18] *Report of Consultant Committee on General Business Expectations*, p. 148.

mathematical trends, cyclical or harmonic analysis of the residuals from trend, and simple or multiple correlation of different series.[19] Because of their conceptual simplicity, statistical indicators have the greatest attraction for the noneconomist since they imply that if A goes up, then B will follow. Whether economic life is that simple is another matter.

[19] See Bibliography: Statistical Methods, p. 55.

CHAPTER 4

Systematic Techniques
of Forecasting

Systematic forecasting derives from the classic approach of economic theory—the discovery of cause-effect relations among different economic factors, which hold for past, present, or future. The use of systematic methods for forecasting requires all the theoretical training, knowledge of institutional and statistical facts, technical skill, and social and political insight that an economist can command. The economist who tackles the forecasting problem today has three great advantages over economists working a generation ago.

The first advantage is the development of modern economic theory, which has made rapid progress since the Great Depression. Prior to the 1930s, economic theory was fragmented into separate theories of wages, money, international trade, public finance, and so forth, but lacked an overall structure for linking up the various theories. The continuing development of economic theory in the past few decades has greatly advanced economists' understanding of how the major elements in a nation's economy are interrelated.

The second advantage is the existence of several systems of national accounting, which present a comprehensive statistical picture of the national economy. The major systems are (1) GNP, which measures national income and output; (2) input-output, which estimates technological relations among different industries, and (3) flow of funds, which focuses on the role of money and credit in the productive process. The three systems should not be viewed as competitive but as complementary. They are described in detail in Chapter 5.

The third advantage is the availability of high-speed electronic computers which permit economists to handle far more data and more complex interrelationships than was formerly possible.

By using modern economic theory and data from systems of national accounts, as well as other data and information, economists are developing forecasting techniques of various degrees of rigor and complexity. The less mathematical (though not necessarily less complex) techniques leave more room for the judgments or instincts of the analyst and for the use of non-quantitative—even noneconomic—information. The more rigorous approach involves the construction of econometric models, which may require difficult mathematical and statistical procedures.

The model-building approach can be applied to short- and long-term general economic forecasting and to many more limited business problems, such as the future demand for particular products. Models need not, however, be forbiddingly difficult to be useful. In this chapter some simplified models for several types of forecasting problems are presented.

The Intuitive Approach

It is difficult to find a word that exactly describes the approach to systematic forecasting which, while it makes use of economic theories, national accounting, and other statistical techniques, does not produce forecasts by exact mathematical techniques. We have called this approach "intuitive," though the analyst's conclusions, obviously, do not rest solely upon his intuitions. Probably the best term to describe it is that coined by Sidney Alexander, of the Massachusetts Institute of Technology, who named it "the lost horse method"—after the old joke about how to find a lost horse. (Go to where the horse was last seen and ask yourself where you would go if you were a horse.)

In general business forecasting, each component of the gross national product—consumption expenditures, domestic investment, foreign investment, and government expenditures—is regarded as a lost horse. The analyst starts by noting where these variables were last reported by the U.S. Department of Commerce and the route they followed to get there. But how the analyst answers the question of where each component of GNP will go from there, how deeply he probes beneath these vast aggregates to discover the cause of their behavior, how he handles the complex interrelations among them (since none is independent of the others), how and to what extent he introduces political, psychological, or other factors that may affect the economy, will depend upon his skill, patience, insight, forecasting talent, and information.

A conscientious analyst will take apart each element in the economic system to get the most detailed picture possible of its operation. He will study federal government plans and policies, study political pressures to weigh the likelihood of the passage of important pieces of legislation and attempt to estimate the price tags they will bear, study trends in state and local expenditures, estimate probable government revenues under various assumptions, and attempt to gauge coming developments in money, credit, and lending policies. He will go behind domestic investment to study the factors affecting the capital programs of particular industries, the probable output of the capital goods industries, the likely course of inventories and the ratios between inventories and sales and production and capacity. He will study the factors that affect building construction, such as the ratio of the housing inventory to the number of households, credit terms, availability of mortgage money, vacancy rates, rents, and price movements. He will measure his investment analysis against the findings of the capital spending surveys of the Securities and Exchange Commission–Department of Commerce, McGraw-Hill, and the National Industrial Conference Board, and check these further by what he learns from businessmen or other economists in particular industries, in government, and in universities or research institutions.

The competent economist will try to gauge people's probable consumption expenditures by studying movements in wages and salaries, debt repayment obligations, cash and other liquid asset holdings, the stock of durable consumer goods, and their age distribution. He will try to get a line on innovations or model changes, model introduction dates and schedules, trends in advertising expenditures, and shifts in public tastes or ways of living.

He will study population growth, trends in the age composition of the population, changes in the spatial location of the population. He will try to figure out how noneconomic factors, like international relations, threats of conflict or easing of tensions, and national political elections may affect people's spending intentions. He will brood about changes he detects in the buying mood of his wife, his neighbors, and whomever he meets or reads about. He will check his feeling about the tone of business with many observers, and weigh his judgment against the findings of the expectational surveys. He will study international developments, estimate their probable effects on United States imports and exports and upon capital movements, anticipate the effects of United States economic and military aid programs—and of foreign governments' aid programs—consider the effect of tariffs, quantitative restrictions, various countries' inflationary or deflationary monetary developments, and trends in the supply and price of raw materials.

The analyst must put all these parts together to make a whole, but he must also have a conception of how the whole is likely to affect the separate parts. He will finally want to test his conclusions about the coming shape of GNP and the likelihood of a change in its course against the conclusions of other economists, government officials, and business leaders.

Since the task of preparing a forecast of the national economy can be a virtually endless one, in view of the plethora of statistical and other information available, the economist must figure out the point at which he has all the information he can handle, given the staff he has to assist him. He may also, if he is a business economist, consider the implications of his forecast for company policies and programs and take cognizance of the public relations effect of his forecast, either upon the officers of his company or, if his forecast is to be widely distributed, upon the general public. Such "political" considerations, though they should not affect the substance of his conclusions, may have a considerable effect upon the manner in which he presents them.

The economist, in preparing his forecast, will be working hard against time—not only because his report will be needed for early use but also because he will want to base his forecasts on the most recent information; if he takes too long, his facts will grow cold. Most business economists have discovered that the best procedure is to stay at the forecasting job continuously, always modifying the forecast on the basis of fresh information.

The test of whether an economist has done a good forecast is, of course, not its comprehensiveness, its brilliance of style or logic, or its public relations effect, but how it comes out. Forecasts done in the manner suggested—or in any manner—cannot be expected to be consistently accurate. If done conscientiously, however, they should be a useful summarization of the main factors that management will want to consider. A good forecast will give management a comprehensive view of the main elements in the business picture, together with the logical inferences about the data that a reasonable and well-trained man can draw. Management does not expect precognition or second sight in an economist, but it does expect his best judgment as to what all the evidence implies.

The Econometric Approach

The more rigorous way of tackling the forecasting problem is to build an econometric model. The term "econometric" refers to an analytical technique that combines the disciplines of economics, mathematics, statistics, and accounting. The econometric model-builder tries to make explicit and exact his assumptions and logical processes, whereas the lost-horse or intuitive analyst may leave his assumptions and logic implicit or vague.

The work of the econometrician may seem incomprehensible to businessmen because of its mathematical and theoretical complexity; but at a time when many outstanding corporations have come to use complicated mathematical techniques for solving industrial and management problems, the work of the econometrician need not be neglected simply on the grounds of difficulty.

Every econometric model is based upon a theory or set of theories about what will determine general business activity or the specific industrial situation being forecast. Econometricians can invent or borrow their theories from the history of economic doctrine. When the econometrician has formulated the theory of his forecast, he must translate it into a set of mathematical equations. These equations will relate what he wants to find out (the dependent, or endogenous, variables) to what he already knows or can estimate (the independent, or exogenous, variables); this set of equations is his model.

This description can best be understood by the presentation of a simple five-equation model of the national economy:

$$C = aY + b \qquad (1)$$
$$I = cP_{-1} + d \qquad (2)$$
$$T = eG \qquad (3)$$
$$G = C + I + E \qquad (4)$$
$$Y = G - T \qquad (5)$$

where C stands for consumption; I, investment; T, taxes; G, gross national product; Y, national income; P_{-1}, previous year's profits; and E, government expenditures. The small letters, $a \ldots e$, are statistically determined constants, called parameters, which make the equations balance.

The meaning of each of the above equations is as follows:

Equation (1) means that people's expenditures for consumer goods and services will depend on how much they earn—or, stated mathematically, consumption is a function of income.

Equation (2) means that next year's investment is a function of this year's profits.

Equation (3) means that taxes will be a function of future gross national product.

Equation (4) is a definitional equation, which simply means that GNP equals consumption plus investment plus government expenditures.

Equation (5) is another definitional equation, which means that national income equals GNP minus taxes.

All five equations, taken together, constitute our forecasting model. To prepare the model for use, one must first look up the statistics on consumption, national income, investment, profits, taxes, and gross national product over a series of years. From these records, values must be calculated for the parameters a, b, c, d, and e to make each of the first three functional equations come out about right in any given year.

We have estimated the parameters for these equations and have substituted them in our model which looks as follows:

$$C = 0.7Y + 50 \qquad (1)$$
$$I = 0.9P_{-1} + 30 \qquad (2)$$
$$T = 0.2G \qquad (3)$$
$$G = C + I + E \qquad (4)$$
$$Y = G - T \qquad (5)$$

This is now a working model that can forecast values of C, I, T, G, and Y once P_{-1} and E have been estimated. The way the model is set up, it is necessary to solve it each time the values of P_{-1} and E change. Since the model is relatively simple, the changing of values is not a problem, but in more complicated models, it would be a time-consuming process. What the econometrician does is to get a general solution of the model in which each endogenous variable depends only on the exogenous variables. Then it is a simple matter to get different forecasts with different values of the exogenous variables. This general solution, which is sometimes called the "reduced form," is also useful for analytical purposes since the impact of a change in one of the exogenous variables on the endogenous variables can be estimated. For example, with the reduced form, it is possible to say how much a given increase in government spending will increase the GNP.

Although our model can be solved easily, it is useful to see how the reduced form is obtained. First, if any endogenous variable depends only on the exogenous variables, for example, I in equation (2), I can be expressed in terms of the exogenous variable and this relationship can be used whenever I appears in the rest of the model, such as in equation (4). This process serves to reduce the number of equations and simplifies the process of solution.

The next step is to transfer all the endogenous variables to the left side of each equation and leave all the exogenous variables and constants, if any, on the right side. For convenience, let the exogenous variable in each equation be represented by X_i. The equations now become:

$$
\begin{aligned}
C - 0.7Y &= 50 &&= X_1 &&(1) \\
T - 0.2G &= 0 &&= X_2 &&(2) \\
G - C &= E + 0.9P_{-1} + 30 &&= X_3 &&(3) \\
Y - G + T &= 0 &&= X_4 &&(4)
\end{aligned}
$$

The problem, now, is to solve for C, T, G, and Y in terms of X_1, X_2, X_3, X_4. The process used is called matrix inversion. It is a cumbersome process, but can be done quickly on a computer.[1] The reduced form of the model is as follows:

$$G = 2.27X_1 - 1.59X_2 + 2.27X_3 + 1.59X_4 \quad\quad (1)$$
$$Y = 1.82X_1 - 2.27X_2 + 1.82X_3 + 2.27X_4 \quad\quad (2)$$
$$T = .45X_1 - 1.32X_2 + .45X_3 + .32X_4 \quad\quad (3)$$
$$C = 2.27X_1 - 1.59X_2 + 1.27X_3 + 1.59X_4 \quad\quad (4)$$

Now values of C, I, T, G, and Y can be forecast, given any particular assumptions about the values of P_{-1} and E. (Note that $I = 0.9P_{-1} + 30$.) Assuming that corporate profits this year are running at $60 billion and that federal, state, and local government spending next year is budgeted to run at $130 billion, the value of investment next year can be found from the equation noted above. Its value will be $84 billion. Then, turning to the reduced form of our equations, the value of X_1 is 50. Both X_2 and X_4 are zero, but X_3 now becomes 214 (130 + 0.9(60) + 30). Substituting these values in the reduced form, the gross national product next year will be $600 billion; national income, $480 billion; tax receipts, $120 billion; and consumption, $386 billion. Had this year's profits been assumed to be $90 billion and next year's federal, state and local government expenditures to be $200 billion, investment next year would be $111 billion, consumption $509 billion, national income $656 billion, tax receipts $164 billion, and gross national product, $820 billion.

The above model has, of course, been presented strictly for didactic purposes. It is based on the simple assumption that next year's gross national product depends upon this year's

[1] A good, simple example of matrix inversion is given in Katherine Harding's *Basic Properties of Matrix Algebra*, Bureau of Mines Information Circular 8332 (Washington, D.C.: U. S. Department of the Interior, 1967). A worthwhile text on matrix algebra especially for economists is Clopper Almon, Jr.'s *Matrix Methods in Economics* (Reading, Mass.: Addison-Wesley, 1967).

profits and next year's government spending. No model can be better than the theory on which it is based.

It must be emphasized that even if a model is "good," in the sense of correctly relating the important variables, it does not follow that it will produce correct forecasts, for every model includes exogenous variables that must be estimated by the forecaster. If wrong assumptions are made about key exogenous variables, such as government spending, taxes, monetary policy, or other critical factors, no model, however sound, can yield correct forecasts. The test of a good model is to see whether, when the actual exogenous variables are inserted, the model yields reasonably accurate "forecasts." The most important and difficult work in econometric forecasting—as in a more intuitive approach—is the effort to specify the right exogenous variables affecting the economy (or the model). Reporting and judgment play a crucial role in determining the basic assumptions for the forecast.

Although theoretically and mathematically more complex than the simple model presented above, actual econometric forecasting models have essentially the same structure. In the large models, the number of variables and equations may run into the dozens or even into the hundreds; and the equations may be nonlinear, rather than linear as in our simple model. Yet all econometric models are based on the same fundamental principle that certain relations among economic variables are sufficiently stable to be used for forecasting and that certain known variables will determine future economic activity.

To be sure, the relations among economic variables will never be completely stable; this is the nature of economic activity in the real world. But the important question is whether the relations will be stable enough, within some range of probable error, to be used in a forecast. If it turns out that there is insufficient stability in any relationship, it means that the theory on which the equation was based had something wrong with it. Econometrics can thus be a useful device for discarding useless theories. If all economic theories are useless in the sense indicated, then economics, as it is known, is a complete waste of time.

In fact, some economists do maintain that relations among economic variables are too unstable to provide a basis either for historical analysis or for forecasting. However, others suggest that, though relations of economic variables are too unstable to be used in econometric models, they are still useful, as theories, for intuitive types of analysis. This would appear to be a *non sequitur*. The econometric use of a fuzzy concept may reveal its insubstantiality; a "literary" approach may conceal the theory's insubstantiality, but not improve its usefulness.

In any case, all of economic theory—mathematical or literary—is based on the assumption of reasonably stable relations among different economic factors. If this assumption did not have significant truth in it, the making of economic theories would long since have ceased. More than that, if the real world did not exhibit considerable stability among economic causes and effects, all attempts to make policy rationally, in business or government, would be impossible.

Econometric model-builders are often criticized because they perform highly complex operations upon data that are so rough as not to permit such manipulation. The critics argue that errors in the data may often be considerably greater than what the econometric forecast is supposed to show. This is a serious matter, but, once again, it is a problem that does not affect only econometricians; poor data can spoil the analysis of any economist. The econometrician may, however, contend that the testing of data by model analysis can point up the need for more and better statistics. Econometricians feel that the Biblical injunction, "Seek and ye shall find," applies to the improvement of economic statistics.

Other criticisms leveled at econometric methods are that they are based on static, not dynamic, theories; that they deal

in huge, meaningless aggregates, like consumption and investment, instead of with the markets for particular goods; that
they ignore social, political, and other noneconomic factors
that can affect a forecast; that they imply a false sort of "economic man" and do not allow for the actual psychological
motivations of human beings, which can result in important
economic changes. Econometricians are not dismayed by such
criticism. In response to the essentially technical criticisms
that their models are static, rigid, or weak on money and prices,
or insufficiently refined in detail, and the like, they go ahead
and try to get the bugs out of their models—to build more
dynamically, build in more monetary elements, go behind the
large aggregates and study particular sectors and industries,
reduce rigidities, and so forth.

Responding to the charge that econometric models are inherently mechanical, naive, clumsy, and insensitive to political,
social, or psychological factors, Lawrence Klein, an econometrician at the University of Pennsylvania, replies, "Econometrics recognizes that social behavior is exceedingly complex
and that a limited number of variables related together in
fairly simple and elegant equations cannot explain the whole
of such behavior . . . [but] the econometrician is no less flexible than any other historian who tries to evaluate the future
on the basis of the past."[2] In summary, the great argument for
econometric models is that they provide a superior means of
organizing the complicated materials of economics, of system-
atizing the whole forecasting process, of providing straight-
forward conclusions, and, afterward, of discovering what may
have gone wrong in a forecast and, thereby, profiting from
past mistakes. The usefulness of models is not limited to government or scholarly research. Forecasting models can also serve
business. Some large corporations are making serious use of

[2] Lawrence R. Klein, *A Textbook of Econometrics* (Evanston, Ill.: Row,
Peterson, 1953), p. 3.

them. Moreover, their use has spread with the growth of modern computer technology.

Models for Business Use

In 1962, Lawrence Klein wrote, "To build a realistic model of the American economy requires a year in data collection and preparation, another year in estimation with much experimentation following both false and fruitful leads, and finally years more of testing the model, applying it to practical problems. Every two or three years the model must be revised to keep it up to date. The magnitude of the effort involved is a definite drawback to the approach."[3] While the complexities of the models now being developed have increased markedly, the continued advances in the technology of computers, the experience of those working with the machines, and particularly the growing acceptance of the idea of group efforts in solving these problems has made the econometric approach much more flexible than originally thought.

Klein himself has been a pioneer in bringing about cooperation between business and academic economists in building and developing a realistic model of the United States economy. Several years ago, a few economists from leading business firms independently approached Klein, who was teaching at the Wharton School of Business at the University of Pennsylvania, for academic assistance in building econometric models. Rather than consulting on an individual basis, Klein conceived the idea of a group effort through which individual business firms would support academic research related to an econometric model. The business economists have met

[3] Lawrence R. Klein, *An Introduction to Econometrics* (Englewood Cliffs, N.J.: Prentice-Hall, 1962), p. 269.

quarterly with Klein and his colleagues to discuss the problems of the model and to prepare forecasts. The "control" solution of the Wharton model is the result of the combined thinking of the Wharton faculty and business economists of the participating firms. In addition, each business economist is free to use the model in his own work. Over the years the number of business firms seeking to support the project has increased to such an extent that a new approach has become necessary. The Wharton Economic Forecasting Unit has provided a remote access system through which an individual subscriber can use the Wharton model. As a result, an up-to-date, short-term econometric forecasting model that is relatively easy to use will be available to the general public at a reasonable cost.

The Wharton model is a relatively large-scale, sophisticated model that quarterly forecasts the gross national product. It is used primarily to forecast eight quarters ahead. The model includes fifty-one structural equations plus thirty-two identities. There are fifty exogenous variables, but many of these are items that can easily be estimated. The exogenous variables that are more difficult to estimate are government spending, world trade, and monetary factors.[4]

Another large-scale model that has benefited from the joint participation of business and academic economists is that of the Interindustry Forecasting Unit of the University of Maryland. The Maryland model forecasts long-run, full-employment gross national product together with the purchases and sales (inputs and outputs) of ninety-three industries. The Maryland input-output model is conceptually simple, but, because of the great amount of industrial detail it includes, the model can only be worked on a computer. Like the Wharton model, the Maryland model requires a great deal of judgment on the part of the forecaster, who must make estimates

[4] A complete description of the model is available in Michael K. Evans and Lawrence R. Klein, *The Wharton Econometric Forecasting Model*, 2d ed. (Philadelphia, Penn.: University of Pennsylvania Press, 1968).

of such critical variables as government expenditures and exports.

Basically, the Maryland model sets up four structural relationships to describe the changing technological structure and functioning of the American economy: (1) changes in consumer spending on individual commodities per dollar of change in income; (2) capital spending on new plant and equipment required per dollar of sales increase by individual industries; (3) amount of labor required in each industry per dollar of sales; and (4) material requirements per dollar of sales of each industry. This last factor is the input-output matrix—a table listing the purchases of every industry from other industries and the sales of every industry to other industries.

The value of the Maryland model is its ability to break down broad movements in the American economy into specific projections for each industrial sector. Maryland's Interindustry Forecasting Unit regularly analyzes the impact of changing economic or political conditions, such as a major technological development or a reduction in defense activities, on the American economy and on particular industries. The Maryland and Wharton models[5] are undoubtedly only forerunners of other large-scale econometric models for business use in this age of the computer. Recently a number of private firms have developed models of their own.

Highly sophisticated econometric techniques need not be employed, however, to produce long-term projections of the national economy or to select particular industries that will be of some help to companies in planning their capital spending and expansion programs. Some skeptics maintain that long-range projections are merely a rationalization of the basic optimism of the American businessman. But there is a more fundamental reason for business's interest in such pro-

[5] Reports on forecasts of both the Maryland and Wharton models are regularly published in *Business Week*. See the listing of *Business Week* in Part III of this book, Index of Source Materials.

jections: Large corporations are finding it increasingly necessary to plan their investment programs well into the future.
When McGraw-Hill first started surveying the outlook for
plant and equipment spending in 1948, less than half of the
companies reporting had any real investment plans; in 1969
nine out of ten companies included in the survey had plans
for at least four years ahead. Many companies have accepted
the principle that if they do not expand, they may shrink, for
in the highly competitive American business environment, it
is seldom possible to stand still. To determine how much they
should expand, managements want long-range projections that
will give them some guidance—however rough—to the future
demand for their products. For large industrial producers such
projections of their markets depend primarily upon the general
outlook for the national economy.

Most long-term projections of the gross national product are
based on a simple growth model showing what our economy
is capable of producing if past trends in productivity persist
and a growing labor force is fully employed.[6] A projection
based on such a model for the United States in the period
from 1969 to 1975 is presented in Table 4 together with actual
data from 1962 to 1968.

The important assumptions of a growth model are:

1. An increase in productivity—usually the average long-
   term rate of increase in the past.
2. A moderate decline in the number of hours worked.
3. Full employment.
4. A growth in the demands of the various sectors of the
   economy great enough to consume the increased supplies.
   (This assumption implies acceptance of what is popularly
   called Say's law—supply creates its own demand. But most
   of our economic problems arise because supply does not
   always create its own demand. In accepting Say's law, a

[6] An excellent reference for long-term projections is *Long-Range Economic
Projection,* Studies in Income and Wealth (Princeton, N.J.: Princeton University Press for National Bureau of Economic Research, 1954), Vol. 16.

Table 4 *Long-Term Economic Growth*

	Civilian Employment* (in millions)	*Average Hours per Week†*	*Man-hours per Year‡ (in billions)*	*GNP per Man-hour§*	*GNP, in 1958 Dollars (in billions)*
Actual					
1962	66.7	38.7	129.1	$4.10	529.8
1963	67.8	38.8	131.5	4.19	551.0
1964	69.3	38.7	134.1	4.33	581.1
1965	71.1	38.8	137.9	4.48	617.8
1966	72.9	38.6	140.7	4.68	658.1
1967	74.4	38.0	141.4	4.77	674.6
1968	75.4	37.8	142.5	4.97	707.6
Projected					
1969	77.0	37.6	144.8	5.12	741.3
1970	78.8	37.4	147.4	5.27	777.0
1971	80.3	37.2	149.4	5.43	811.2
1972	81.8	37.0	151.3	5.59	845.8
1973	83.3	36.8	153.3	5.76	883.0
1974	84.7	36.6	155.0	5.93	919.2
1975	86.4	36.4	157.2	6.11	960.5

* Based on U.S. Bureau of Census population estimates. Assumes 3.5 percent unemployed.
† Average weekly hours for total nonagricultural private economy.
‡ Column 1 x column 2 x 50 weeks.
§ Increases 3 percent a year from 1968 on.

long-term growth model eliminates one of the key problems in economic life today.)

In addition, other general limitations of a simple, long-term growth model should be noted:

1. The projection represents a normal level of output that could be attained for the period projected. The deviations from this level may be wide in any given year.
2. The base year from which the projection is made is usually assumed to be an average or normal year.
3. Because the model is essentially an extrapolation of past trends, important structural changes that may occur in the future cannot be taken into consideration.

In spite of such limitations and qualifications, long-range projections can be meaningful. They can be used to illustrate what continued growth will mean in terms of the increases in demands of the various sectors of the economy or in terms of increased leisure. They can also be used in formulating government policies that would be beneficial to the growth of the economy. It should be noted, however, that a projection of long-term growth does not imply any specific policy.[7]

The task of moving from overall projections of the national economy to the outlook for the markets of particular products in which an individual company is interested requires the forecaster to make a massive search for relevant marketing and technological information and to engage in a great deal of guessing. Whatever the scope of the data base, the complexity of the model, or the availability of information about impending technological change, business forecasting also depends upon the intuition and judgment of the forecaster. Great stress must be made that there is no conflict between econometrics and intuition. Each reinforces the other. There is also no simple or consistent formula for combining these elements. A businessman, in a particular case, may rightly be guided by his intuition alone concerning the market for a product, especially where consumer acceptance is the critical variable. But, in any case, he will also be wise to weigh the implications of econometric analysis of the demand for his product.

Econometric techniques are well-adapted to the problem of forecasting the demand for many particular products. The fundamental demand equation is $D = f(p)$ where D is the demand, f is a symbol representing a function, and p is the price of the quantity demanded. The equation merely says

[7] A number of long-term projections have been published. The National Planning Association, a private organization, regularly projects economic trends ten years ahead. Detailed information on these projections is available to subscribers of *National Economic Projections*. The staff of the Joint Economic Committee also prepares long-term projections. Their most recent projection was published in *U.S. Economic Growth to 1975: Potentials and Problems* (Joint Economic Committee, Washington, D.C.: Government Printing Office, 1966).

demand is a function of price. For some commodities, it is desirable to include other variables besides price, for example, time, population, prices of competitive goods, and so on. There are many complex statistical problems involved in demand functions;[8] however, business analysts who wish to estimate the demand for a certain product can usually make a creditable guess by using simple statistical techniques of regression analysis. Since most demand functions are more nearly logarithmic than linear, the analysis is usually carried out in terms of the logarithms of the variables.

The demand for nondurable goods is relatively simple. Thus, the demand for wheat depends essentially on the price of wheat alone; or the demand for beer upon the retail price of beer, the income of consumers, and the average retail price level of all other commodities. But the demand for durable goods is more complicated because in most cases the demand is a derived one. Thus, the demand for new automobiles depends in part on the existing stock of automobiles; or the demand for steel is critically dependent upon the total level of industrial production in the economy.

In a pioneer study Roswell H. Whitman found that a good way of estimating the demand for steel was to make it a function of the price of steel, the rate of change of steel's price, and the index of industrial production.[9] And Roos, in studies of the demand for many durable consumer goods, including automobiles, refrigerators, and washing machines, based his demand forecasts on five factors: (1) "supernumerary income" —that is, income in excess of basic living costs; (2) number of households; (3) consumers' stocks; (4) prices; and (5) credit

[8] See Henry Schultz, *The Theory and Measurement of Demand* (Chicago: University of Chicago Press, 1938); Mordecai Ezekiel, *Methods of Correlation Analysis,* 2d ed. (New York: Wiley, 1941); G. J. Stigler, "The Limitations of Statistical Demand Curves," *Journal of the American Statistical Association,* 34 (September 1939), 469 ff.; and especially Gerhard Tintner, *Econometrics* (New York: Wiley, 1952).
[9] Roswell H. Whitman, "The Statistical Law of Demand for a Producers' Good," *Econometrica,* 4 (April 1936), 138–152.

conditions as measured by months to pay.[10] Roos forecast producers' demands for capital goods on the basis of (1) new corporate purchasing power—mainly retained corporate profits, new corporate financing, and capital consumption allowances for depreciation, obsolescence, and so forth; (2) the long-term interest rate; and (3) the ratio of prices of consumer goods to prices of capital goods.[11]

No single formula will be appropriate for forecasting the demand for all types of products, since the characteristics of goods and markets vary so widely. But the above examples may suggest several ways of approaching the problem of forecasting product demand. In cases where consumer taste and acceptance are the critical factors, the businessman should depend more upon the market researchers and his own judgment, as noted above, than upon his economists.

Many specific business forecasting problems, other than the future demand for particular products, can be handled or at least clarified by using econometric techniques similar to those mentioned above. For instance, econometric methods can be used to forecast changes in costs, prices, interest rates, inventories, and so on. In every case, the problem is that of selecting factors upon which the element being forecast appears to depend and then testing the past relationships of factors to discover a formula that will have forecasting value. An analysis revealing the factors that make for change will also reveal much about the policies or decisions a business firm should adopt with respect to pricing, selling effort, and purchasing, in order to increase its profits.

[10] C. F. Roos, "Survey of Economic Forecasting Techniques," *Econometrica*, 23 (October 1955), 388–389.
[11] *Ibid.*, pp. 390–391.

SELECTED BIBLIOGRAPHY

Statistical Methods

Croxton, Frederick E., and Dudley J. Cowden. *Applied General Statistics*. 2d ed. New York: Prentice-Hall, 1955.
———. *Practical Business Statistics*. 3rd ed. New York: Prentice-Hall, 1960.
Davis, Harold T. *The Analysis of Economic Time Series*. Bloomington, Ind.: The Principia Press Inc., 1941.
Fox, Karl A. *Intermediate Economic Statistics*. New York: Wiley, 1968.
Suits, Daniel B. *Statistics: An Introduction to Quantitative Economic Research*. Chicago: Rand McNally, 1963.
Wallis, W. Allen, and Harry V. Roberts. *Statistics: A New Approach*. Glencoe, Ill.: Free Press, 1956.

Deterministic Techniques of Forecasting

Adams, F. Gerard. "Consumer Attitudes, Buying Plans, and Purchases of Durable Goods: A Principal Components, Time Series Approach," *Review of Economics and Statistics*, 46 (November 1964), 347–355.
Foss, M. "Manufacturers' Inventory and Sales Expectations," *Survey of Current Business*, 41 (August 1961), 25–31.
Friend, Irwin, and F. Gerard Adams. "The Predictive Ability of Consumer Attitudes, Stock Prices and Non Attitudinal Variables," *Journal of the American Statistical Association*, 59 (December 1964), 987–1005.
Juster, F. Thomas. *Anticipations and Purchases: An Analysis of*

Consumer Behavior. Princeton, N.J.: Princeton University Press, 1964.

————. *Consumer Buying Intentions and Purchase Probability: An Experiment in Survey Design.* Occasional Paper No. 99. New York: Columbia University Press for National Bureau of Economic Research, 1966.

————. "Some Experimental Results in Measuring Purchase Probabilities for Durables, and Some Tentative Explorations of Time-Series Demand Models," *A.S.A. 1967 Proceedings of the Business and Economic Statistics Session* (Washington, D.C.: American Statistical Association, 1967), pp. 87–96.

Maynes, E. Scott. "An Appraisal of Consumer Anticipations Approaches to Forecasting," *A.S.A. 1967 Proceedings of the Business and Economic Statistics Session* (Washington, D.C.: American Statistical Association, 1967), pp. 114–123.

McNeil, John M., and Thomas L. Staterau. "The Census Bureau's New Survey of Consumer Buying Expectations," *A.S.A. 1967 Proceedings of the Business and Economic Statistics Session* (Washington, D.C.: American Statistical Association, 1967), pp. 97–113.

Mueller, Eva. "Ten Years of Consumer Attitude Surveys: Their Forecasting Record," *Journal of the American Statistical Association,* 58 (December 1963), 899–917.

Okun, Arthur. "The Predictive Value of Surveys of Business Intentions," *American Economic Review Papers and Proceedings,* 52 (May 1962), 212–225.

Tobin, James. "On the Predictive Value of Consumer Intentions and Attitudes," *Review of Economics and Statistics,* 41 (February 1959), 1–11.

Universities–National Bureau Committee for Economic Research. *The Quality and Economic Significance of Anticipations Data.* Special Conference Series, Vol. 10. Princeton, N.J.: Princeton University Press for National Bureau of Economic Research, 1960.

Symptomatic Techniques of Forecasting

Broida, Arthur L. "Diffusion Indexes," *American Statistician,* 9 (June 1955), 7–16.

Friedman, Milton, and Anna Jacobson Schwartz. *A Monetary History of the United States, 1867–1960.* Studies in Business Cycles No. 12. Princeton, N.J.: Princeton University Press for National Bureau of Economic Research, 1963.

Moore, Geoffrey H. (ed.). *Business Cycle Indicators.* 2 vols. Princeton, N.J.: Princeton University Press for National Bureau of Economic Research, 1961.

———. "Forecasting Short-Term Economic Change," *Journal of the American Statistical Association,* 64 (March 1969), 1–22.

———, and Julius Shiskin. *Indicators of Business Expansions and Contractions.* Occasional Paper No. 103. New York: Columbia University Press for National Bureau of Economic Research, 1967.

Shiskin, Julius. *Signals of Recession and Recovery.* Occasional Paper No. 77. New York: National Bureau of Economic Research, 1961.

Sprinkel, Beryl W. "Monetary Growth as a Cyclical Predictor," *Journal of Finance,* 14 (September 1959), 333–346.

Systematic Techniques of Forecasting

METHODS

Beach, E. F. *Economic Models: An Exposition.* New York: Wiley, 1957.

Butler, William F., and Robert A. Kavesh (eds.). *How Business Economists Forecast.* Englewood Cliffs, N.J.: Prentice-Hall, 1966.

Christ, Carl F. *Econometric Models and Methods.* New York: Wiley, 1966.

————. "Econometrics and Model-Building," *The Annals of the American Academy of Political and Social Science,* 370 (March 1967), 164–175.

Evans, Michael K. *Macroeconomic Activity, Theory, Forecasting, and Control.* New York: Harper & Row, 1969.

Klein, Lawrence R. *An Introduction to Econometrics.* Englewood Cliffs, N.J.: Prentice-Hall, 1962.

————. *A Textbook of Econometrics.* Evanston, Ill.: Row, Peterson, 1953.

Lewis, John P. "Short-term General Business Conditions Forecasting —Some Comments on Method," *Journal of Business,* 35 (October 1962), 343–356.

————, and Robert C. Turner. *Business Conditions Analysis.* 2d ed. New York: McGraw-Hill, 1967.

Maisel, Sherman J. *Fluctuations, Growth and Forecasting: The Principles of Dynamic Business Economics.* New York: Wiley, 1957.

Organization for Economic Co-operation and Development. *Techniques of Economic Forecasting: An Account of the Methods of Short-term Economic Forecasting Used by the Governments of Canada, France, Netherlands, Sweden, U.K. and U.S.* Introduction by C. W. McMahon. Paris: The Organization, 1965.

Suits, Daniel B. "Forecasting and Analysis with an Econometric Model," *American Economic Review,* 52 (March 1962), 104–132.

MODELS FOR FORECASTING

Almon, Clopper, Jr. *The American Economy to 1975—An Interindustry Forecast.* New York: Harper & Row, 1966.

Christ, Carl F. "Aggregate Econometric Models: A Review Article," *American Economic Review,* 46 (June 1956), 385–408.

Cromarty, W. A. "An Econometric Model for United States Agriculture," *Journal of the American Statistical Association* (September 1959).

Duesenberry, James S., Otto Eckstein, and Gary Fromm. "A Simulation of the United States Economy in Recession," *Econometrica,* 28 (October 1960), 749–809.

————, Gary Fromm, Lawrence R. Klein, and Edwin Kuh (eds.).

The Brookings Quarterly Econometric Model of the United States. Chicago: Rand McNally, 1965.

Evans, Michael K., and Lawrence R. Klein. *The Wharton Econometric Forecasting Model.* 2d ed. Philadelphia, Penn.: University of Pennsylvania Press, 1968.

Fisher, Malcolm R. "A Sector Model—The Poultry Industry of the U.S.A.," *Econometrica,* 26 (January 1958), 37–66.

Friend, Irwin, and Paul Taubman. "A Short-term Forecasting Model," *Review of Economics and Statistics,* 46 (August 1964), 229–236.

Freund, William C., and Edward D. Zinbarg. "Application of Flow of Funds to Interest-Rate Forecasting," *Journal of Finance,* 18 (May 1963), 231–248.

Gallaway, Lowell E., and Paul E. Smith. "A Quarterly Econometric Model of the United States," *Journal of the American Statistical Association,* 56 (June 1961), 379–383.

Galper, Harvey, and Edward Gramlich. "A Technique for Forecasting Defense Expenditures," *Review of Economics and Statistics,* 50 (May 1968), 143–155.

Houthakker, Henderick S., and L. D. Taylor. *Consumer Demand in the United States, 1929–1970.* Cambridge, Mass.: Harvard University Press, 1966.

de Leeuw, Frank, and Edward Gramlich. "The Federal Reserve–M.I.T. Econometric Model," *Federal Reserve Bulletin,* 54 (January 1968), 11–40.

Liebenberg, Maurice, Albert A. Hirsch, and Joel Popkin. "A Quarterly Econometric Model of the United States: A Progress Report," *Survey of Current Business,* 46 (May 1966), 13–26.

Murphy, Frank P. "Input-Output and the Company," *A.S.A. 1967 Proceedings of the Business and Economic Statistics Section* (Washington, D.C.: American Statistical Association, 1967), pp. 9–12.

Smith, Paul E. "An Econometric Growth Model of the United States," *American Economic Review,* 53 (September 1963), 682–693.

Stone, Richard, and D. A. Rowe. "The Market Demand for Durable Goods," *Econometrica,* 25 (July 1957), 423–443.

Thurow, Lester C. "A Fiscal Policy Model of the United States," *Survey of Current Business,* 49 (June 1969), 45–64.

Valavanis-Vail, Stefan. "An Econometric Model of Growth, U.S.A., 1869–1953," *American Economic Review*, 45 (May 1955), 208–227.

Evaluation of Forecasts

Evans, Michael K., Yoel Haitonsky, and George I. Treyz. "An Analysis of the Forecasting Properties of U.S. Econometric Models." Paper delivered at National Bureau of Economic Research Conference on Econometric Models of Cyclical Behavior, November 1969.

Fels, Rendigs, and Hinshaw, C. Elton. *Forecasting and Recognizing Business Cycle Turning Points*. New York: Columbia University Press for National Bureau of Economic Research, 1968.

Okun, Arthur M. "A Review of Some Economic Forecasts for 1955–57," *Journal of Business*, 32 (July 1959), 199–211.

Stekler, Hermon O. "An Evaluation of Quarterly Judgmental Economic Forecasts," *Journal of Business*, 41 (July 1968), 329–339.

———. "Forecasting with Econometric Models: An Evaluation," *Econometrica*, 39 (July–October 1968), 437–463.

Zarnowitz, Victor. *An Appraisal of Short-Term Economic Forecasts*. Occasional Paper No. 104. New York: Columbia University Press for National Bureau of Economic Research, 1967.

PART II

---

*Data for
Business Forecasting*

CHAPTER 5

National Accounting
Systems

Among the most important data the business forecaster uses are three major national accounting systems: (1) gross national product and income accounts, (2) input-output accounts, and (3) flow of funds accounts.

Gross National Product and Income Accounts

From the standpoint of the business analyst, the first and most important of the three major systems of national accounts is organized around the concept of the gross national product. This system was developed by the U.S. Department of Commerce and the National Bureau of Economic Research in the 1930s and has been continuously refined. Basic research on national accounting systems has also been in progress for some time in many foreign countries and the use of these systems is now widespread, particularly among industrial countries.

The GNP system regards national output and income from three standpoints: as a receipts total, as an expenditures total, and as a total value of production. These three totals are identical, since every expenditure is simultaneously a receipt; and all the goods and services produced, if valued at their sales prices, also equal receipts or expenditures.

Gross national product attempts to measure the dollar value of final goods and services currently produced. It is called "gross" because it includes depreciation charges. Final products, rather than intermediate products, are measured to avoid double counting. For example, in the production of a loaf of bread, only the final cost of bread is counted and the values of wheat and flour that have been used up in the course of production are not counted separately. Since only current production is measured, neither the purchase nor the sale of existing houses or shares of stock is included. These are merely exchanges of existing assets.

Total production of goods and services is divided into four groups: government purchases of goods and services; gross private domestic investment; personal consumption expenditures; and net exports of goods and services. Government purchases include all federal, state, and local government expenditures except those for interest and social security measures, which are excluded on the grounds that they are not payment for the current production of goods and services. Gross private domestic investment consists of expenditures for residential housing, new plant and facilities, and the net change in business inventories. Personal consumption expenditures include all purchases by individuals and nonprofit institutions for goods and services other than new residential building. Personal consumption expenditures also include some nonmonetary transactions, such as the imputed value of food provided free to employees, food produced and consumed on the farm, and the value of rent in owner-occupied homes. Net exports of goods and services are equivalent to the net sales of goods and services abroad.

National income attempts to measure the aggregate earnings before taxes of labor and property that arise from the current production of goods and services. National income plus depreciation charges, excise taxes, and a few other minor items theoretically equals gross national product, for the latter represents the value of production and the former the charges against it. In practice, however, there is usually a discrepancy between the two totals due to statistical difficulties of measurement.

National income is broken down into compensation of employees, proprietors' and rental income, net interest, and corporate profits. Corporate profits included in national income exclude inventory profits or losses. This adjustment is necessary because only the value of the *real* change in inventories is counted as current output in the gross national product.

In the compilation of gross national product and income totals, several other important measures are derived that are useful in economic discussions and analyses. Some of these can be described briefly.

Personal income includes wages and salaries and other labor income; rents, interest, dividends, and transfer payments; and income from farming, professional work, and other unincorporated businesses. It includes income accruing to non-profit organizations and private trust, pension, and welfare funds. Not all income need be received in the form of money. About 1 percent of personal income represents payments in kind—food, clothing, and lodging. Moreover, personal income includes so-called imputed income, such as the estimated return that owner-occupants of dwellings could theoretically have realized if they offered their houses for rent. Imputed incomes normally amount to about 3 percent of total personal income. Personal incomes are calculated before the payment of federal, state, and local income taxes.

Disposable personal income is equal to personal income after deducting personal income taxes.

Personal consumption outlays include personal interest payments and personal transfers to foreigners in addition to personal consumption expenditures.

Personal savings are equal to disposable personal income less personal consumption outlays. The savings figure, being a residual figure, is subject to errors in both totals from which it is derived. It is perhaps the most unreliable of the major national income figures and should be used with caution.

Sources

Survey of Current Business especially the annual July issues and *National Income Supplements; Economic Indicators.*

Input-Output Accounts

A second national accounting system, based upon so-called input-output analysis, has been developed by Wassily W. Leontief of Harvard University. Leontief's basic idea was to construct a table—like the *tableau economique* of the eighteenth century French physiocrats—to show the way goods flow from one industry to another (in Leontief's terminology, the input and output of each industry). The table describes the interrelations of all parts of the economy and provides a basis for studying how disturbances to the system would be absorbed or aggravated by the various economic sectors.

The conceptual relationship between national income and product accounts and input-output accounts is illustrated in Table 5, which shows the production accounts of a set of industries and the rearrangement of these accounts into a consolidated income and product account table and an input-output table. The product (receipts) side for these production accounts shows the sale of goods to each intermediate industry, in addition to sales to final users. The expense side shows the consumption of intermediate goods by each industry as well as the value added by each industry.

In the simplified example in Table 5, there are only three industries—A, B, and C. Industry A provides raw materials to B and C and also sells to individuals. Industry B sells to C, to individuals, and to the government. Industry C sells only

Table 5 *Relationship Between Income Product Accounts and Input-Output Accounts*

Part I: Industry Production Accounts

Expenses and Profits		Receipts	
Industry A			
Wages	80	Sales to industry B	20
Depreciation	5	Sales to industry C	30
Profits	15	Sales to persons	50
	100		100
Industry B			
Purchases from industry A	20	Sales to industry C	10
Wages	25	Sales to persons	25
Depreciation	5	Sales to government	25
Profits	10		
	60		60
Industry C			
Purchases from industry A	30	Sales to persons	60
Purchases from industry B	10		
Wages	15		
Profits	5		
	60		60

Part II: National Income and Product Account

Wages	120	Personal consumption	
Profits	30	expenditures	135
Depreciation	10	Government	25
GNP	160	GNP	160

Part III: Input-Output Table

		A	B	C	Persons	Government	Total
Inter-	A		20	30	50		100
mediate	B			10	25	25	60
	C				60		60
Value	Wages	80	25	15			120
added	Other	20	15	5			40
		100	60	60	135	25	XXX

Intermediate   Final demand

SOURCE: "The 1958 Interindustry Relations Study," unpublished document, U.S. Department of Commerce, November 1964, p. 3.

to individuals. In Part I, each industry's receipts from sales are shown in the right-hand column and expenses and profits are in the left-hand column.

In Part II of the table, those elements of the operation of industries A, B, and C that represent components of gross national product and national income are brought together. In Part III, all the information displayed in Parts I and II has been rearranged in the form of an input-output table. Along the row marked A is industry A's sales to B and C and to individuals. Similarly, rows B and C show their respective sales to other industries, to individuals, and to government. The columns indicate the purchases of industries A, B, and C from other industries and their value added. The sum of the final demand columns (persons and government) equals gross national product. The value-added rows for each industry show the gross national product originating in that industry.

If only the intermediate part of the input-output table is considered, it looks like a chart for a supergame of tic-tac-toe. Every square or "cell" in the tic-tac-toe grid simultaneously stands for either an input or an output. From the standpoint of its position in the column, the number in a cell is an input to the industry named at the top of the column. From the standpoint of its position in a horizontal row, the same number represents an output of the industry named at the left of the row. The total inputs and outputs of each industry in the columns and rows will always be identical. The point of this construction, then, is to show what every industry sells to every other industry to further its production.

Once the basic input-output table has been constructed, setting forth the statistics for a particular year, it must be made operational—that is, capable of being used to show the way fresh developments will affect the whole system. This is done by translating the original table into a so-called input-output coefficient table, which provides the numerical relationships between inputs and outputs. The input coefficients are calculated by dividing each cell in an industry's column by the output of that industry. The coefficients will be large or small depending on how important particular inputs are in producing particular outputs.

When the table or matrix is to be used repeatedly for solving different problems, it is useful to "invert" the matrix. Then, by changing the values of the outputs of particular industries —for instance, to take account of the effect of producing an extra $100 million worth of airplanes or of substituting transistors for vacuum tubes or of subtracting 10 million tons of steel production—the analyst can work back to see what effect the new development will have on the sales and production of all industries.

Sources

Leontief, Wassily. *The Structure of the American Economy 1919–1939.* New York: Oxford University Press, 1941.

———, et al. *Studies in the Structure of the American Economy.* New York: Oxford University Press, 1953.

"The 1958 Interindustry Relations Study." Unpublished document, U.S. Department of Commerce, November 1964.

"The Interindustry Structure of the United States," *Survey of Current Business,* 44 (November 1964), 10–29.

"Construction Activity in the 1958 Input-Output Study," *Survey of Current Business,* 45 (May 1965), 13–24.

"The Transactions Table of the 1958 Input-Output Study and Revised Direct and Total Requirements Data," *Survey of Current Business,* 45 (September 1965), 33–49, 56.

"Personal Consumption Expenditures in the 1958 Input-Output Study," *Survey of Current Business,* 45 (October 1965), 7–20, 28.

"Additional Industry Detail for the 1958 Input-Output Study," *Survey of Current Business,* 46 (April 1966), 14–17.

"Industrial Impact of the 1966 Housing and Commercial Building Decline," *Survey of Current Business,* 46 (November 1966), 11–12.

Input-Output Transactions: 1961, Staff Working Paper in Economics and Statistics, No. 16. U.S. Department of Commerce, July 1968.

Flow-of-Funds Accounts

A third system of national accounts called the flow of funds was developed by the economists at the Federal Reserve Board following the pioneering research of Morris A. Copeland. The flow of funds, as the name implies, concentrates on the transfer of funds among economic sectors rather than on income and production. In a way, the flow of funds can be looked at as a deconsolidation of the savings and investment account in GNP. All of the transfers of funds that were netted out to arrive at savings and investment in nonfinancial terms are included.

Flow-of-funds data are 'presented in matrix form. The columns are sectors or decision-making groups that transact the national business. In the most detailed tables, these sectors include the following twenty categories: households; farm business; nonfarm noncorporate business; corporate nonfinancial business; state and local governments; U.S. government; rest of world; monetary authorities; commercial banks; savings and loan associations; mutual savings banks; credit unions; life insurance companies; other insurance companies; private pension funds; finance companies; security brokers and dealers; open-end investment companies; agencies of foreign banks; and banks in U.S. territories and possessions. The rows of the matrix are the transactions; these include both nonfinancial and financial transactions. Nonfinancial transactions include savings and investments or capital outlays. Financial transactions are divided broadly into five categories: monetary reserves; deposit claims on financial institutions; insurance and pension reserves; credit market instruments; and other claims. Each of these categories is further subdivided. In all, there are approximately forty different types of financial categories. The highly simplified model of the flow-of-funds matrix shown in Table 6 illustrates some of the basic features of this system of accounts.

Table 6   *Flow-of-Funds Matrix*
(Hypothetical data in billions of dollars)

Transactions	Private, Domestic, Nonfinancial		Government		Financial Intermediaries		Rest of World		Totals	
	USE	SOURCE	USE	SOURCE	USE	SOURCE	USE	SOURCE	USE	SOURCE
Nonfinancial										
Saving		179		−10		5		−4		170
Capital outlays	170								170	
Financial										
Net financial investment	9		−10		5		−4		0	
Total financial uses and sources	· 69	60	5	15	70	65	3	7	147	147
Deposits at financial intermediaries	50		3			55	2		55	55
Loans and securities	19	60	2	15	70	10	1	7	92	92

NOTE: This table compresses twenty sectors in the full system into four columns for sector types, and the rows similarly group the full list of transaction categories.

SOURCE: Board of Governors of the Federal Reserve System, *Flow of Funds Accounts, 1945–1967* (Washington, D.C.: Federal Reserve Board, February 1968), p. I.10.

For the economy as a whole (column entitled "Totals"), savings must equal capital outlays, and, since all financial transactions are borrowings (sources) from one sector and lendings (uses) to another, net financial transactions must be zero. In each financial market, borrowings must equal lendings. In any one sector, such as the private, domestic, non-financial sector, savings equal capital outlays and net financial investment. Net financial investment for each sector is the difference between uses and sources or between borrowings and lendings. In addition to the overall matrix, there are tabular presentations showing summary national totals of funds raised in credit markets as well as flows through financial intermediaries to credit markets.

The flow-of-funds system, though still relatively new, promises to be a valuable addition to the collection of tools available to the business forecaster. Until recently, analysis of the national economy has been split, for all practical purposes, between the approach of the economist and that of the financial analyst. The economist's approach has been based upon the gross national product, which measures the market value of the current output of goods and services but cancels out many expenditures, such as money spent on already existing assets or on services and materials that do not constitute final products, transactions in securities, mortgages and other forms of debts and financial assets.

The financial approach, which has been primarily concerned with such data as money in circulation, bank deposits, government and corporate securities, has had no means of relating these financial facts to the "real" economic activities within the economy—that is, to the production of goods and services, which is the concern of GNP analysis. In actuality, of course, "real" economic events have powerful effects upon the financial sector of the economy, and financial developments powerfully affect "real" economic developments. The flow-of-funds accounts now provide a means of linking up the financial and nonfinancial information about the U.S. economy. They are an important aid to the business analyst for forecasting general price movements, tracing the probable effects on different sectors of the economy of tax cuts or changes in business or consumer spending, and discovering weak and strong points in the financial picture.

Sources

Flow of Funds Accounts, 1945–1967. Federal Reserve Board, February 1968; *Federal Reserve Bulletins.*

CHAPTER 6

Population and Labor Force

Population

Population information, so vital to long-range economic forecasting, is available in excellent detail from the U.S. Bureau of the Census. Additional government and private compilations are available to supplement this information.

The most complete information on total U.S. population is available in the decennial census taken since 1790. The Bureau of the Census, U.S. Department of Commerce, provides data for intercensal years. Since 1940, the Bureau of the Census has conducted a monthly population survey, currently sampling 50,000 households. The survey was designed primarily to measure unemployment, but now provides information on such subjects as changes in the number of households, family composition, doubling up of family groups, marital status, education, migration, incomes, and plans for consumer expenditures.

The Bureau of the Census has an extensive program for projecting almost all the important demographic variables, such as total population, population by age groups, births, deaths, marriages, household formation, school attendance, and labor force.[1]

---

[1] A summary of recent projections is provided in *Current Population Reports,* Series P-25, No. 388 (March 14, 1968).

The Office of Vital Statistics of the U.S. Department of Health, Education and Welfare publishes data on births, deaths, marriages, and divorces.

Sources

Population—Census; Current Population Reports; Monthly Vital Statistics Report; Vital Statistics—Special Reports—National Summaries.

Labor Force, Employment, and Unemployment

Each month the Bureau of the Census estimates the labor force, employment, and unemployment for the U.S. Bureau of Labor Statistics (BLS). In addition to overall figures, details on characteristics of employed and unemployed persons, hours worked, and duration of unemployment are presented. These data are based on a sample of about 50,000 households and are therefore subject to the error found in most polls involving relatively small samples. Moreover, some of the answers gathered by the poll takers depend on the subjective judgments of the respondents concerning their status as employed or unemployed. Some people may be anxious to work, but, unless they report that they have actively sought employment in the survey week, they are excluded from both the labor force and the unemployed totals. The monthly estimates of employment and unemployment would probably be changed appreciably by moderate changes in definitions.

Current population survey data provide the only comprehensive figures covering employment status of the population. They are published promptly and the unemployment data in particular are used as a current indicator of the general health of the economy.

Sources

Employment and Earnings and Monthly Report of the Labor Force; Monthly Labor Review.

Labor—Insured Employment

The Bureau of Employment Security (BES), U.S. Department of Labor, publishes weekly data on claims for benefits under employment security programs. These data provide the most up-to-date information on current trends in unemployment. Geographic detail is available. However, the limitations of these data should be kept in mind. Certain groups of workers are excluded from employment security programs, including self-employed persons, unpaid family workers, and new entrants into the labor market. In a period when unemployment is substantial and of long duration, the extent of exhaustion of benefits may have an important bearing on the magnitude of insured employment totals.

Persons working only a few hours during the week are sometimes eligible for unemployment compensation but are counted as employed in the census estimates. A woman who may have withdrawn from the labor force under the census definition may still be eligible for unemployment benefits.

Source

Unemployment Insurance Claims.

Labor—Nonagricultural Employment

The Bureau of Labor Statistics publishes monthly data on employment in nonagricultural establishments. Estimates are published for more than 200 separate industry groups and subgroups. These data are useful as indicators of changes in economic activity in various sectors of the economy.

Source
Employment and Earnings and Monthly Report of the Labor Force.

Labor—Earnings

The Bureau of Labor Statistics publishes data on average hourly and weekly earnings and straight-time hourly earnings for employees in nonagricultural employment. Average hourly and weekly earnings include payments for overtime and are useful indicators of trends in purchasing power. The series on straight-time hourly earnings is useful as a measure of trends in wage rates.

Source
Employment and Earnings and Monthly Report of the Labor Force.

Labor—Hours

The Bureau of Labor Statistics publishes average weekly hours of employees in nonagricultural establishments. Changes in economic activity are frequently reflected in the number of hours worked before they are reflected in aggregate employment and unemployment totals. Hence, changes in hours worked are considered a useful anticipatory series.

Source
Employment and Earnings and Monthly Report of the Labor Force.

Productivity

Productivity is one of the most important factors in the growth of the American economy and is basic to increasing living standards. Measures of changes in productivity are essential to the analysis of a wide range of problems besides economic growth, such as employment opportunities, wages, hours, and increased earnings.[2]

Productivity is simply the ratio of output to input, but since there are many ways of defining output and input, several different measures of productivity are theoretically possible. The most widely used ratios are those that relate output to man-hours. It is important to realize that such a ratio does not mean that labor is the source of all productivity. The rate of technological development and improvement in plant layouts and processes are some of the factors that affect the productivity ratio defined as output per man-hour. Productivity is essentially a long-term movement, and changes in any one quarter or any one year may therefore be misleading. An index of total output per man-hour is affected by shifts from low to high productivity industries; thus, if a farm worker goes to

[2] An excellent reference on productivity is John W. Kendrick, "National Productivity and Its Long-Term Projection," *Long-Range Economic Projection Studies in Income and Wealth* (Princeton, N.J.: Princeton University Press, 1954), 67–104.

work in a steel mill, productivity will rise. Overall productivity indexes are useful in making long-term projections of the economy.

The Bureau of Labor Statistics currently publishes data on productivity for the total private economy, agriculture, non-agricultural industries, total manufacturing, and selected industries.

Sources

Handbook of Labor Statistics; Monthly Labor Review.

CHAPTER 7

Business Investment And Construction Activity

Business Investment Capital Spending

Business investment in plant and equipment is an important dynamic factor in determining the level of total economic activity. Data are available from a variety of sources.

PLANT AND EQUIPMENT EXPENDITURES

Perhaps the most widely used data on business capital outlays is the series on plant and equipment expenditures put out jointly by the U.S. Department of Commerce and the Securities and Exchange Commission (SEC). This series estimates new plant and equipment expenditures by all United States businesses except agriculture. Capital outlays charged to current expense, such as hand tools, are excluded. Data are available from 1945. This series is popular because the SEC and the Department of Commerce also estimate anticipated outlays on the basis of reports from a sample of companies. Because of the importance to the general economy, information on businessmen's plans for capital expenditures is extremely useful in forecasting total economic activity.

In addition to the government series on planned capital

outlays, there are the McGraw-Hill surveys which are made twice a year and reported in *Business Week*. A preliminary survey made each fall covers anticipated outlays for the next two calendar years and a final survey covering anticipated outlays for the next four years is made in the spring. The McGraw-Hill estimate is based on a sample that is smaller than the SEC–Department of Commerce sample, but it is available earlier and contains additional information, such as longer-term perspective and supplementary data on factors affecting investment decisions. A useful summary of the records of both government and McGraw-Hill surveys in projecting actual capital outlays can be found in the Report of the Consultant Committee on Plant and Equipment Expenditure Expectations by the Subcommittee on Economic Statistics of the Joint Committee on the Economic Report.

Another private source of anticipatory information on plant and equipment spending is the series on capital appropriations by large manufacturers and investor-owned utilities published jointly by the National Industrial Conference Board and *Newsweek*.

Sources

Report of the Consultant Committee on Plant and Equipment Expenditure Expectations; *Survey of Current Business; Business Week; The Conference Board Record; Newsweek*.

NONRESIDENTIAL FIXED INVESTMENT

The series on Nonresidential Fixed Investment from the national income and product accounts is the sum of Producers Durable Equipment and Nonresidential Construction. It differs from the plant and equipment series in that it includes capital outlays by agriculture and outlays charged to current expense. The series Producers' Durable Equipment includes new equipment expenditures by all U.S. business and agriculture except heavy immovable equipment installed on site. Nonresidential Construction includes industrial, commercial, farm, public utility, oil- and gas-well drilling expenditures, and, in addition, the value of heavy immovable equipment installed on site.

Source
Survey of Current Business.

MACHINERY AND ALLIED PRODUCTS
INSTITUTE'S CAPITAL OUTLAYS

A less widely used concept of capital outlays, but one that is particularly useful to the producers of capital equipment, is that of the Machinery and Allied Products Institute. This concept includes new plant and equipment outlays by U.S. business and government, and foreign purchases of U.S. equipment. It also includes expenditures for maintenance and repair.

Source
Capital Goods Review.

Construction Activity

Data on residential construction and public construction as well as business construction activity are available in a variety of forms: permits, contracts, expenditures, and units.

PERMITS

The U.S. Bureau of Labor Statistics publishes monthly data on building construction authorized by local building permits including residential and nonresidential building and additions and alterations.

Sources

Construction Review; Current Construction Reports (Series C-40).

CONTRACTS

The McGraw-Hill Information Systems Company (formerly the F. W. Dodge Corporation) publishes data on valuation and area of contracts. The *Engineering News-Record* also has a contract series for heavy construction. These data are generally considered to be a useful indication of future levels of construction activity.

Sources

McGraw-Hill Information Systems Company, *Engineering News-Record; Federal Reserve Bulletin; Survey of Current Business.*

EXPENDITURES

The U.S. Department of Commerce prepares comprehensive expenditure for all types of construction activity, both private and public, residential and nonresidential. Private construction expenditures are used in the gross national product statistics. Forecasts of construction activity are prepared each fall for the following year.

Sources

Construction Review; Current Construction Reports (Series C-30).

NONFARM RESIDENTIAL UNITS

The series on the number of nonfarm residential units started, compiled by the U.S. Bureau of the Census, is a useful indicator of the volume of residential construction.

Sources

Construction Review; Current Construction Reports (Series C-20).

OTHER CONSTRUCTION DATA

Data on costs, prices, and the like, are reported in *Engineering News-Record* and *Construction Review*. New advance planning of heavy construction and a cumulative backlog of plans are reported by *Engineering News-Record*. Other construction data can be found in the *Dodge Reports, Dodge Bulletins,* and *Dodge Construction Statistics* released by the McGraw-Hill Information Systems Company.

CHAPTER 8

Production And Trade

Aggregate indexes of industrial production and output levels of single industries are useful indicators of the state of the economy. Industrial figures are available weekly and monthly, agricultural figures less frequently.

Production

INDUSTRIAL PRODUCTION

The Federal Reserve monthly Index of Industrial Production (1957 to 1959 = 100) is designed to measure changes in the physical volume of output of manufacturing and mining industries and utilities which produce about 35 percent of the value of total production of goods and services in the United States. Important areas of the economy not covered by the index are construction activity, transportation, trade, services, and agriculture. In addition to the monthly index which relies heavily on man-hour data as a measurement of output, the Federal Reserve Board compiles an annual index based on more comprehensive data from such sources as manufacturing censuses. Only 4 percent of the annual index is based on man-hour data. Each year the monthly series are checked against the annual indexes and revised accordingly.

The monthly index is useful as an aggregate measure of economic activity. Because of the exclusion of some of the more stable components of the total economy, such as services, fluctuations in the index tend to be wider and more frequent than for the economy as a whole.

A detailed description of the Federal Reserve Board index, including historical data on the 1957 to 1959 = 100 base, is available in the Federal Reserve Board publication, *Industrial Production, 1957–1959 Base.*

Sources

Federal Reserve release, "Business Indexes" (G.12.3); *Federal Reserve Bulletin; Survey of Current Business; Economic Indicators; Business Conditions Digest.*

INDUSTRIAL PRODUCTION—WEEKLY INDICATORS

There are a number of weekly series available on important aspects of industrial production. These series are useful as current indicators but are subject to erratic fluctuations not shown in comparable series covering longer time periods. The *Business Week* Index gives a weekly picture of changes in industrial production. The following series are reported in *Economic Indicators;* in addition, weekly releases are available from the sources listed:

Bituminous Coal Products, Bureau of Mines, U.S. Department of the Interior
Cars and Trucks Assembled (Motor Vehicles), Ward's Reports, Inc.
Electric Power Output, Edison Electric Institute
Freight Car Loadings, Association of American Railroads
Paperboard Production, National Paper Board Association
Steel Production, American Iron & Steel Institute

AGRICULTURAL PRODUCTION AND MARKETING

The U.S. Department of Agriculture compiles four indexes of the physical volume of farm output. Only one, the Index of Physical Volume of Farm Marketings (1957 to 1959 = 100), is available monthly. The others, Volume of Farm Marketing and Home Consumption, Farm Output and Gross Farm Production (all 1957 to 1959 = 100), are published annually.

Sources

Agriculture—Situation and Outlook Reports: Farm Income Situation; *Agricultural Statistics.*

Trade

Trade statistics and information are available from numerous government and private sources. The data vary in timeliness from potential sales and orders to actual sales and inventories. The information may be classed in five categories.

TOTAL SALES AND INVENTORIES

Total sales and inventories for manufacturing and trade are estimated monthly by the U.S. Department of Commerce. These data are useful indicators of the level of economic activity at various stages of production. Sales reflect demand for goods and services while inventories reflect the difference between output and consumption of the economy. The data are revised frequently as additional information becomes available.

Sources

Survey of Current Business; Economic Indicators.

MANUFACTURERS' SALES, INVENTORIES, AND ORDERS

In addition to total sales and inventories, the Department of Commerce collects data on new and unfilled orders of manufacturers, which are useful anticipatory statistics. Estimates of sales and inventories are based on a sample of some 2,000 manufacturers representing approximately 60 percent of total manufacturers' sales. The orders sample is somewhat smaller. Data are available monthly from 1939 to date. Beginning in 1961, data on manufacturers' inventory and sales expectations have become available.

Sources

Current Industrial Reports: Manufacturers' Shipments, Inventories and Orders; Survey of Current Business: U.S. Department of Commerce News Release, Manufacturers' Inventories and Sales Expectations.

WHOLESALE SALES AND INVENTORIES

Data on wholesale sales and inventories are based on a sample of about 4,000 wholesale establishments and are available monthly from 1939.

Sources

Monthly Wholesale Trade Report; Survey of Current Business: U.S. Department of Commerce News Release, Manufacturing and Trade Inventories and Sales.

RETAIL SALES AND INVENTORIES

Monthly statistics from a large number of diversified retail stores, including independent, chain, and department stores, as well as mail-order outlets have been collected since 1935 by the Department of Commerce and published monthly. Beginning in 1962, data are also available weekly.

Since a large proportion of consumer expenditures are made at retail stores (outlays for many services constituting an important exception), the retail sales series is a significant barometer of consumer demand. This is not a precise measure but is the best available on a monthly and weekly basis.

Sources

Advance Retail Sales Report; Monthly Retail Trade Report; Weekly Retail Sales Report; Survey of Current Business: U.S. Department of Commerce News Release, Manufacturing and Trade Inventories and Sales.

FOREIGN TRADE

Statistics on exports and imports, trade by countries and the like are published monthly by the Department of Commerce in *Foreign Trade Current Reports.*

Data on balance of payments are reported quarterly in U.S. Department of Commerce News Releases and in the *Survey of Current Business.* Historical data are published in the *Survey of Current Business.*

Data on exchange rates are available on a monthly basis in the *Federal Reserve Bulletin.* Daily quotations on official and free-market exchange rates of many countries can be found in the *New York Times.* Data on unofficial or black-market exchange rates are published in Pick's *Currency Yearbook.*

CHAPTER 9

Commodity Prices

Individual commodity prices are available daily in many newspapers. More important as general economic indicators, however, are the various commodity indexes that are calculated.

Agricultural Prices

The index of prices received by farmers is based on the average price of fifty-five farm products. The index is published monthly and is based on 1910 to 1914 = 100. The index of prices paid by farmers is currently based on the average price of over 300 commodities and services used by farmers together with taxes, interest, and wages. The index is published monthly and is based on 1910 to 1914 = 100. The index of parity prices is the ratio of prices received to prices paid. It also is published monthly and is based on 1910 to 1914 = 100.

In addition to the indexes, prices received and parity prices for certain commodities are available. The parity price for an individual commodity is defined by the U.S. Department of Agriculture as "that price for the commodity which will give the commodity a purchasing power with respect to articles that farmers buy equivalent to the purchasing power of such commodity in the base period." In practice, the parity price of most commodities is determined by multiplying the average price of the commodity over the base period years (1910 to 1914) by the current value of the index of prices paid by farmers. The concept of parity has been extremely important in the federal government's agricultural program.

Source

Agricultural Prices.

Consumer Price Index

The U.S. Department of Labor, Bureau of Labor Statistics, publishes a Consumer Price Index (1957 to 1959 = 100). The main purpose of the index is to measure the average change in the prices of goods and services purchased by city wage earner and clerical-worker families. It does not reflect such special price concessions as discounts available to many consumers in periods of declining sales or of overstocking by producers or distributors. Federal excise and state sales taxes are included, but income taxes are not.

In addition to its general economic use, this index is also important in many wage contracts where wages are tied to the "cost of living."

Data are available monthly since 1913.

Sources

Consumer Price Index; Monthly Labor Review; Survey of Current Business.

Wholesale Price Index

The Bureau of Labor Statistics publishes a comprehensive index of wholesale prices (1957 to 1959 = 100). The index currently comprises nearly 2,200 prices of commodities. Prices are collected for a single day of the month, usually the Tuesday of the week containing the fifteenth. Prices for various groups and subgroups are available, and a breakdown by economic sectors is available for the years since 1947. The major categories of the economic sector breakdown are as follows:

All commodities
Crude materials for further processing
Intermediate materials, supplies, and components
Finished goods

Consumer finished goods
Consumer foods
Consumer nondurable
Consumer durable

Producers finished goods
Producers goods for manufacturing industries
Producers goods for nonmanufacturing industries

Data are available monthly since 1912 and annually since 1820.

Sources

Wholesale Price Index and Economic Sector Index; Monthly Labor Review; Survey of Current Business.

Spot Primary Market Prices

The Bureau of Labor Statistics publishes a daily index (1957 to 1959 = 100) and prices in primary commodity markets of a selected group of foods, fibers, metals, and other raw materials (total twenty-two items). The index is a sensitive indicator of price changes, fluctuating much more widely than more comprehensive wholesale and consumer price indexes.

Revised data are available for one day a week from June 1946 through 1951, daily from then on. Data are also available for three special dates—August 15, 1939, December 6, 1941, and August 17, 1945. Earlier data are available on the basis of the old index of twenty-eight items (August 1939 = 100).

Sources

Daily Index Numbers and Spot Primary Market Prices; New York Times.

The *Journal of Commerce* publishes a daily index of sensitive commodities (1947 to 1949 = 100). This index is based on thirty commodities and is available on the following day, whereas the BLS index is not available until the second day.

Source

Journal of Commerce.

Dow Jones & Company compiles a daily spot commodity price index (1924 to 1926 = 100) to be used in conjunction with their Commodity-Features Index.

Sources

Wall Street Journal; Barron's.

Commodity Futures

Dow Jones calculates a daily index of future prices of twelve commodities. A commodity futures contract is a legal document to deliver or accept a definite quantity of a particular commodity during a specified calendar month at an agreed price.

Sources

Wall Street Journal; Barron's.

CHAPTER 10

Finance

Economic indicators are available from financial sources. The government's activities and those of the Federal Reserve System are frequently described in newsletters. Private sources are also available. The data cover domestic as well as international transactions.

Business Failures and Incorporations

Number and current liabilities of industrial and commercial failures and new business incorporations are estimated by Dun & Bradstreet. These data on business failures have been available on a monthly basis since 1900; data on new business incorporations, on a monthly basis, go back only to 1945. The data are seasonally adjusted by the National Bureau of Economic Research and are considered useful indicators of trends in general business activity.

Sources

Business Failures; New Business Incorporations; Business Conditions Digest.

Consumer Credit

Consumer credit statistics are prepared by the Federal Reserve Board and cover short- and intermediate-term credit in total and by major types. In addition to the amount outstanding, the volume of credit extended and repaid during each month is also given. Data are available from 1929 to date by months.

Consumer credit is important as a source of consumer purchasing power and is especially significant in the demand for durable goods. In 1968 the amount of installment credit extended was about $95 billion or about 17.5 percent of total personal consumption expenditures. The volume of credit extensions represents additions to the purchasing power stream, while the volume of repayments represents withdrawals.

Sources

Federal Reserve Bulletin and Federal Reserve releases, especially G-19, Consumer Credit.

Debt

The *Survey of Current Business* publishes annual data on public and private debt (net and gross). Separate detail for federal, state, and local governments, corporations, nonfarm mortgage debt, and individual and noncorporate debt is given. Data are available generally from 1919 to date. Latest data are published annually in the *Survey of Current Business*, usually in May.

Source

Survey of Current Business.

Federal Government Finance

Data on financial operations of the federal government are compiled primarily by the U.S. Department of the Treasury and published in the *Annual Report of the Secretary of the Treasury,* the *Treasury Bulletin,* the *Daily Statement of the United States Treasury,* and the *Monthly Statement of Budget Receipts and Expenditures.* The annual *Budget of the United States,* issued by the U.S. Bureau of the Budget, presents comprehensive and detailed statistics including data on obligations, appropriations, and the like.

The "unified budget" is a comprehensive statement of the federal government's financial plan. It was introduced in the *Budget of the United States, Fiscal 1969* (January 1968) and is popularly known as "The Budget." It replaces the old administrative and cash budgets. Receipts and expenditures in the unified budget are now generally presented on a cash basis, but will eventually be presented on an accrual basis.[1]

Sources

Treasury Bulletin; Monthly Statement of Budget Receipts & Expenditures; Economic Indicators.

The national income budget summarizes receipts and expenditures of the federal government as recorded in the national accounts. Primary differences between the national

[1] For a detailed description of the unified budget, see *Report of the President's Commission on Budget Concepts* (Washington, D.C.: Government Printing Office, 1967).

income budget and the unified budget are: (1) on the receipts side, taxes are on an accrual basis not a collections basis, and (2) on the expenditure side, spending is recorded when delivery is made to the government, and purchases and sales of existing real and financial assets are excluded.

Source

Economic Indicators; Survey of Current Business.

The high-employment budget is an estimate of the national income accounts budget at full employment. It is a useful concept to measure the impact of fiscal policy.

Source

Federal Reserve Bank of St. Louis, *Federal Budget Trends.*

State and Local Government Finances

Current data on state and local government finances are published by the Governments Division of the U.S. Bureau of the Census. National totals, by type of government, are published annually for governmental revenue, expenditure, and debt.

Source

Governmental Finances.

Corporate Profits

There are several series of corporate profits, all different in concept and coverage.

STATISTICS OF INCOME

The most complete data on corporate profits are published by the U.S. Department of the Treasury, Bureau of Internal Revenue. On the basis of corporate tax returns, profits and losses as reported for tax purposes of all corporations are tabulated both by size, as measured by net income and assets, and by industry groups. Profit and loss statements, and balance sheet items are also given for a large number of companies. Figures on most items are available annually since 1909 when the corporate tax was first enacted. The definition of profits has varied in accordance with the current revenue acts; nevertheless, by adjusting for changes in definitions, with the supplementary data given, a fairly homogeneous series of corporate profits before and after taxes for all corporations since 1909 can be obtained. Because of the detailed work involved in summarizing the corporate tax returns, the complete data for any particular year are not available until three to four years later.

Source
Statistics of Income.

NATIONAL INCOME—DEPARTMENT OF COMMERCE

For national income purposes, estimates of corporate profits are based on the data from *Statistics of Income.* Because of the time-lag in publication of these data, the U.S. Department of Commerce estimates current profits on the basis of year-to-year changes as shown in samples of large corporations and in data collected from the Interstate Commerce Commission, Federal Power Commission, and the Treasury. These current estimates are revised when the statistics of income data are published.

The national income definition of profits differs from the current tax definition. The chief difference is the exclusion in the national income series of intercorporate dividends and capital gains and losses.[2]

For total corporations and corporations by industries, national income figures are available annually since 1929 for profits before and after taxes, tax liability, dividends, undistributed profits, and inventory valuation adjustments. For total corporations only, these data are available quarterly since 1939.

The statistics of income and national income data on profits are the most comprehensive. The other series commonly used refer almost entirely to profits of manufacturing corporations after taxes. In most of these series, profits are based on quarterly or annual reports of the corporations and may differ from either the tax or national income definitions.

Source

Survey of Current Business.

FEDERAL RESERVE BOARD

The Federal Reserve Board publishes data on sales, profits before and after taxes, and dividends of roughly 200 large

[2] A complete reconciliation between the two series is given in each July issue of the *Survey of Current Business,* National Income and Product Accounts Table 7.5.

manufacturing corporations. The series includes quarterly data beginning in 1946 and annual data beginning in 1939. A breakdown by major industries is available. The Federal Reserve Board also publishes profits before and after taxes for public utility corporations.

Figures for railroads include all Class I line-haul railroads whose net income comprises about 96 percent of all operating revenue in the railroad industry. Income before taxes is available in this series. Figures are given annually since 1929 and quarterly since 1939.

The sample of electric power companies includes twenty-eight of the larger companies in the industry. From 1929 to 1940, this sample covered 26 percent of the operating revenue of all electric power companies having annual revenues of at least $250,000. Earnings before taxes are also available in this series. Figures are available annually since 1929 and quarterly since 1939.

The annual series from 1929 to 1939 for telephone companies includes thirty-three large companies whose net income comprises about 95 percent of the net income of the whole industry. For the quarterly figures beginning in 1939, thirty companies covering 85 percent of all telephone operations are used.

Source
Federal Reserve Bulletin.

FIRST NATIONAL CITY BANK

In April of each year the First National City Bank of New York publishes figures for net income after taxes and net worth of about 3,000 leading corporations for the two preceding years. Roughly half of the corporations are in manufacturing; the remainder include trade, mining, transportation, public utilities service, construction, and finance corporations. The number of companies in the sample varies from year to year but since two years' net income is always reported, the trend of profits of leading corporations can be determined by constructing a chain index.

In addition to publication of annual earnings, the First National City Bank publishes quarterly earnings of about 400 large manufacturing corporations. Like the larger sample, the number of companies varies from quarter to quarter and it is necessary to construct a chain index to determine the trend over any length of time.

Source

First National City Bank Monthly Economic Letter.

SECURITIES AND EXCHANGE COMMISSION

In 1947, the SEC, in conjunction with the Federal Trade Commission, began to issue quarterly financial data for all manufacturing corporations. Condensed balance sheet and profit and loss statements are available by size of corporations and by major industrial groups.

The profit figures reported in the SEC publication differ from the First National City Bank and Federal Reserve data in that they represent estimates of the aggregate of all manufacturing companies and not simply the sum of large or leading companies. The aggregate figures are based on a carefully selected sample. Preliminary investigations of the results indicate that there may be some understatement of the true aggregates, due to incompleteness of the sample. More definitive checks can be made with the statistics of income data.

There are some differences in the concept of SEC profits and the national income profits. The national income series is benchmarked on tabulated profits as reported to the U.S.

Bureau of Internal Revenue, adjusted by eliminating all depletion charges, capital gains and losses, and dividend receipts; but the SEC series recognizes normal depletion charges and dividend receipts and adjusts for capital gains and losses when they are significant in amount. Another important difference is that data used in the national income series are partially consolidated, while the SEC series is based upon consolidated reports.

Source

Manufacturing Corporations—Quarterly Financial Report.

Interest Rates and Bond and Stock Yields

Interest is the price paid for the use of money. In general, it varies with the supply of and demand for money. There is, of course, no one interest rate since the rate depends on the risk and time involved. However, the rate on government bonds often serves as an indicator of other interest rates since these securities are generally considered the least risky. If the rate on government bonds increases, there is usually a corresponding rise in riskier loans.

INTEREST RATES

Data on various kinds of interest rates are available in the *Federal Reserve Bulletin.*

Rates on prime commercial paper. This series represents the cost of open market, short-term credit available to business borrowers of highest credit standing.

Bank rates on business loans. This series covers interest rates charged by selected member banks of the Federal Reserve System on loans to business borrowers.

U.S. government securities. The three-month bill rate measures relatively riskless short-term borrowing. The long-term rate is the generally accepted indicator of interest rates.

CORPORATE BOND YIELDS

Moody's corporate bond yield averages. These are based on selected issues for three groups—railroads, public utilities, and industrials. Data are available from 1919 on a monthly basis and since 1935 on a daily basis. Data are published in *Moody's Bond Survey.*

Standard & Poor's average corporate bond yields. Monthly data are available since 1900, weekly data since 1937. Data are published in *Standard & Poor's Outlook* (weekly) and *Current Statistics* (monthly).

STOCK YIELDS

Both Moody's and Standard & Poor's publish data on dividends and yields of common stocks in the publications listed above. Yields on the Dow Jones stocks are available in *Barron's.*

Sources

Federal Reserve Bulletin; Moody's Bond Survey; Standard & Poor's Outlook; and Standard & Poor's Current Statistics.

Stock Market Prices

There are many averages and indexes of stock prices.
Dow Jones daily stock price averages currently are based on

sixty-five stocks, with separate averages available for thirty industrials, twenty railroads, and fifteen utilities. Data are available back to 1897. Averages are computed for the opening, high, low, and close of each day and by the hour. These averages are useful chiefly for evaluating short-run changes. Because of the method of computation of the averages, they are not particularly good indicators of stock price movements over long periods. In order to adjust for price distortions arising from stock splits, the Dow Jones adjusts the divisor each time a stock is split. The price averages published currently are not the averages of one share of each of the stocks included, but the percentage change shown from day to day is the same as the percentage change in the average price of one share of each stock. Dow Jones averages are perhaps the most widely used of the daily indicators of stock prices.

Sources

Wall Street Journal, for daily information; *Barron's,* for weekly summaries.

Standard & Poor's Daily Stock Price Index (1941 to 1943 = 100) has been based on 500 stocks, 425 industrials, 25 rails, and 50 utilities since February 1957. By linking these series to earlier series based on ninety stocks, daily data are available since 1926. From 1918 to 1926, data are available weekly. Standard & Poor's indexes for all stocks and industrials have been linked with the Cowles Commission Stock Indexes to obtain data back to 1871. The index is computed on the basis of the aggregative index number formula, with the number of shares outstanding as weights. For longer-term trends in stock prices, this index is a better indicator than the Dow Jones, but it is not much better than the Dow Jones in measuring day-to-day changes.

Sources

Standard & Poor's Outlook, for current data; *Standard & Poor's Security Price Index Record,* latest edition, for historical data.

New York Stock Exchange price indexes are published by the New York Stock Exchange. The principal index is the Common Stock Index which is composed of the more than 1,250 common stocks traded on the Exchange. In addition, there are the Financial Index, which includes 75 stocks, the Transportation Index, 76 stocks, the Utilities Index, 136 stocks, and the Industrial Index, which is made up of nearly 1,000 stocks not included in the other three indexes. In addition, the Exchange issues the average price change, which is the change in the Common Stock Index converted into dollars and cents. All five indexes are calculated by the same formula, which is similar to the one used in computing the Standard & Poor's indexes.

The Common Stock Index and the average price change are issued every half-hour, while the financial, transportation, utilities, and industrial indexes are issued every hour. To provide historical data, the Common Stock Index has been linked statistically to the index of 300 common stocks published weekly by the Securities and Exchange Commission from January 7, 1939 to May 28, 1964. Since May 1964 the index is available on a daily close basis. The four industry indexes have been computed daily since December 31, 1965.

Sources

New York Times; Wall Street Journal; New York Stock Exchange.

American Stock Exchange Price Level Index shows the average price change of all common stocks and warrants traded on the American Exchange. It is issued hourly and at the close of trading, and is reported in dollars and cents. The base price for this index was set at $16.88—the average price of all stocks and warrants admitted to dealings on April 29, 1965. Subsequent price levels are obtained by adding or subtracting the average price change to or from the previous index. The average price change is calculated by adding up the price changes of each common stock and warrant since the previous close and dividing that total by the number of stocks and warrants. To account for stock splits, the price change is computed by using the current price and the old price adjusted for the split. When there is a new listing on the Exchange the number of issues used as a divisor is increased by one. A delisting reduces the divisor by one. Data are available from October 1962.

Sources

New York Times; Wall Street Journal; American Stock Exchange.

Savings

Saving is one of the most misunderstood concepts the economist uses. The layman generally thinks of savings as a stock of funds whereas the economist thinks of savings primarily as a flow of funds.

National income and product accounts savings are that part of current income not spent on consumption goods. For the economy as a whole, savings equals investment. For each sector of the economy, there may be differences between savings and investment of that sector. Generally speaking, savings by individuals are greater than investment by individuals, while the reverse is true of business.[3]

The flow-of-funds accounts total savings are defined, as in the national income accounts, as income less consumption expenditures. However, in the flow of funds, consumer durables are not considered as a current consumption expenditure but as an investment. Gross savings in the flow of funds are therefore higher than in the GNP accounts. The flow-of-funds accounts also include information on savings as a stock of funds.

The Securities and Exchange Commission has published annual and quarterly data on Savings by Individuals in the United States since 1933.[4]

The SEC releases contain two concepts of saving. Liquid savings of individuals comprise savings in the form of net increases in currency and bank deposits, saving and loan association shares, equity in private government insurance, securities, and net repayment of mortgage debt and other consumer debt by individuals. Total gross savings consist of liquid savings plus gross savings in the form of nonfarm dwellings and other durable consumer goods. For year-end dates, data are also presented on levels of liquid assets and debts incorporated in liquid savings.

The survey of consumer finances conducted by the Survey Research Center of the University of Michigan provides information on savings. The estimates of consumer savings and

[3] An excellent discussion of this subject can be found in Edward F. Denison, "Saving in the National Economy from the National Income Perspective," *Survey of Current Business* (January 1955). Another good basic reference is *Statistics of Saving*, Report of Consultant Committee on Savings Statistics, organized by the Board of Governors of the Federal Reserve System at the request of the Subcommittee on Economic Statistics of the Joint Committee on the Economic Report (Washington, D.C.: Federal Reserve Board, July 1955).

[4] For estimates of these data back to 1929, see Irwin Friend, with the assistance of Vito Natrella, *Individuals' Savings: Volume and Composition* (New York: Wiley, 1954).

various asset and liability items, or combinations of both, can be related to other information obtained in the survey. Thus, analysis of distribution of savings and of particular assets or liabilities by various characteristics such as income, age, and family composition is possible. The information is based on sample surveys and should be used with care. Reference to the *Statistics of Saving*[5] is suggested for a good description and interpretation of these statistics.

Sources

Survey of Current Business, National Income Supplements, National Income and Product Accounts of the United States, 1929–1965.
Survey of Current Business.
Flow of Funds Accounts, 1945–1967.
Federal Reserve Bulletin.
Survey of Consumer Finances.
Statistical Bulletin.
Goldsmith, Raymond. *A Study of Saving in the United States.* Princeton, N.J.: Princeton University Press, 1955. Gives SEC historical data on total savings from 1897–1949.

Money Supply

The narrow definition of money supply includes demand deposits at all commercial banks other than interbank and government deposits, foreign demand balances at Federal Reserve Banks, and currency held outside the Department of the Treasury, Federal Reserve Banks, and vaults of commercial banks.

The broad definition of money supply includes time depos-

---

[5] Report of the Consultant Committee on Savings Statistics. (Washington, D.C.: Federal Reserve Board, July 1955).

its in addition to the items included in the narrow definition.

Monetary base, as defined by the Federal Reserve Bank of St. Louis, is equal to Federal Reserve credit, the gold stock, Treasury currency outstanding less Treasury deposits at the Federal Reserve, Treasury cash holdings, and other minor items—the total being adjusted for changes in reserve requirements.

The monetary base is a variant on what Friedman, Schwartz, and Cagan call "high-powered money." It is called high-powered because it is essentially money which, if held as bank reserves, may give rise to the creation of several dollars of deposits. Generally speaking, an increase in high-powered money involves an equal percentage increase in the stock of money.

Bank credit proxy is the sum of deposit liabilities of member banks subject to reserve requirements. Since changes in this sum are highly correlated with changes in bank assets, it is used as a proxy for the latter. It is one of the most easily estimated monetary aggregates and is available weekly.

Sources

Federal Reserve Bulletin; Federal Reserve release, "Money Supply and Time Deposits" (H.6); St. Louis Federal Reserve Bank releases, Monetary Trends and U.S. Financial Data.

Friedman, Milton, and Anna Jacobson Schwartz. *A Monetary History of the United States 1867–1960.* Princeton, N.J.: Princeton University Press for National Bureau of Economic Research, 1963.

Cagan, Philip. *Determinants and Effects of Changes in the Stock of Money, 1875–1960.* New York: Columbia University Press, 1965.

Balance of Payments

International financial transactions have become increasingly important for the economy as a whole over recent years, and the business forecaster has found that he must take international considerations into account both in analyzing particular industries and the economy as a whole.

The balance of international payments shows all receipts from foreigners, on one side, and all payments to foreigners, on the other. Receipts from foreigners include payments for exports of goods and services and capital flows resulting from foreign investment in the United States. Payments to foreigners include payments for imports of goods and services, U.S. investment abroad, government loans and gifts abroad, and remittances of U.S. citizens to families abroad.

When the government and citizens of a country spend more abroad than they receive from foreigners, a country is said to have a balance-of-payments deficit. The deficit must be made up by exporting gold, "paper gold," or by reducing one's holdings of foreign exchange. This concept of a deficit and its counterpart, a surplus (an increase in gold, Special Drawing Rights—SDRs, and foreign exchange), are used for global analysis of international transactions. On this basis, total deficits equal total surpluses. Most countries, however, define their balance-of-payments deficits or surpluses in different ways— usually to highlight their specific problems. Canada, for example, often defines her deficit on current account as her balance-of-payments deficit.

The United States currently uses two definitions for a balance-of-payments deficit (or surplus). One, called the liquidity basis, is measured by the decrease (or increase) in U.S. official reserve assets and the increase (or decrease) in liquid liabilities owed to all foreigners. The other, the official reserve transaction basis, is measured by the decrease (or increase) in U.S. official reserve assets and the increase (or decrease) in liquid and certain nonliquid liabilities to foreign official agencies.

While the *net* deficit or surplus position of a country's balance of payments is crucial for policy implications, the business forecaster may also need to analyze the complete system of international receipts and payments. These data are compiled by the Department of Commerce and published in the *Survey of Current Business*. The complete set of accounts are available quarterly about one quarter later. Data on gold and foreign exchange holdings are reported monthly in the *Federal Reserve Bulletin* and additional detail on the capital account is given in the *Treasury Bulletin*.

Sources

Survey of Current Business, May, June, September and December issues; *Federal Reserve Bulletin; Treasury Bulletin.*

PART III

Index Of Source Materials

Index Of Source Materials

Advance Retail Sales Report. Monthly. U.S. Department of Commerce, GPO.* Monthly survey of Bureau of the Census conducted in cooperation with a representative cross section of about 1,700 retail firms which, in total, operate some 35,000 stores in the United States. Advance estimates are preliminary and subject to revision. (See *Current Retail Trade Reports.*)

Agricultural Prices. Monthly. U.S. Department of Agriculture, Statistical Reporting Service, Washington, D.C. 20250. Prices received by farmers for all groups of farm products, index numbers of prices received and paid by farmers, and parity prices.

Agricultural Statistics. Annually. U.S. Department of Agriculture, GPO. Annual compilation of agricultural and related statistics.

Agriculture—Situation and Outlook Reports. Irregularly. U.S. Department of Agriculture, Economic Research Service, Washington, D.C. 20250. Series of periodic reports providing current information on supply, demand, price, and other trends affecting agriculture. In addition to reports on major commodities such as livestock and meat, poultry and eggs, and dairy products, there are reports entitled as follows:

> Farm Income Situation.
> Demand and Price.
> Marketing and Transportation.
> Farm Costs.

* Where GPO is listed as mailing address, items may be obtained from Superintendent of Documents, U.S. Government Printing Office, Washington, D.C. 20402.

Annual Report of the Secretary of the Treasury. Annually. U.S. Department of the Treasury, Washington, D.C. 20220. Gives information on the state of finances for the preceding fiscal year.

Annual Retail Trade Report. Annually. U.S. Department of Commerce, GPO. Annual summary of retail trade. (See *Current Retail Trade Reports.*)

Annual Survey of Manufacturers. Annually. U.S. Department of Commerce, Bureau of the Census, Washington, D.C. 20233. Started in 1949 and continued for those years not covered by the *Census of Manufacturers* (see below). It provides up-to-date statistics on key measures of manufacturing activity for industry groups and important individual industries. For prices and detailed description of data, see *Bureau of the Census Catalog,* which lists all bureau publications.

Banking and Monetary Statistics. Washington, D.C.: Federal Reserve Board of Governors, 1943. Basic reference book for banking, monetary, and certain related financial statistics with back data and explanatory text.

Supplements:

Sec. 1   Banks and Monetary System. 1962.
Sec. 2   Member Banks. 1967.
Sec. 5   Bank Debits. 1966.
Sec. 6   Bank Income. 1966.
Sec. 9   Federal Reserve Banks. 1965.
Sec. 10 Member Bank Reserves and Related Items. 1962.
Sec. 11 Currency. 1963.
Sec. 12 Money Rates and Securities Markets. 1966.
Sec. 14 Gold. 1963.
Sec. 15 International Finance. 1962.
Sec. 16 Consumer Credit. 1965.

Barron's. Weekly. Barron's Publishing Co., Inc., 30 Broad Street, New York, New York 10004. Emphasis is on articles of investment interest. There is a statistical section on stock prices and Dow Jones data.

Bituminous Coal Production. Weekly. U.S. Department of the Interior, Bureau of Mines, Washington, D.C. 20250. Data are daily averages of production of bituminous coal and lignite production.

The Budget of the United States. Annually. Executive Office of the President, Bureau of the Budget, GPO. Detailed budget estimates and special analyses. A review of the budget summarizing congressional action on the President's proposals is usually available in August of each year.

Bureau of the Census Catalog. Quarterly, on a cumulative-to-annual basis plus twelve issues of the Monthly Supplement. U.S. Bureau of the Census, GPO. Listing includes regular reports of the census and unpublished materials (computer tape and punch card data files, and special tabulations).

Business Conditions Digest (formerly *Business Cycle Developments*). Monthly. U.S. Department of Commerce, GPO. Brings together many of the economic time series used by business analysts and forecasters. Includes data on national income and product, business cycle indicators of the National Bureau of Economic Research, and anticipation and intention data.

Business Failures. Weekly. Dun & Bradstreet, Inc., P.O. Box 803, New York, New York 10008. Number of failures in week ending on the previous Thursday; comment and analysis by liability size, industry, geographic regions. Issued Mondays.

Business Men's Expectations. Quarterly. Dun & Bradstreet, Inc., P.O. Box 803, New York, New York 10008. Report and summary of results of 1,500 interviews with businessmen about future expectations concerning their sales, profits, prices, employment, inventory, and new orders.

Business Week. Weekly. McGraw-Hill Publishing Company, Inc., 330 West 42nd Street, New York, New York 10036. Interpretive text and *Business Week* Index plus the series of weekly business statistics, Figures of the Week.

Capital Goods Review. Quarterly; available to members. Machinery and Allied Products Institute, 1200 Eighteenth Street N.W., Washington, D.C. 20036. Statistical studies and interpretive text on various aspects of capital goods production.

Census of Manufactures. U.S. Department of Commerce, GPO. Comprehensive statistics on manufacturing. Censuses are taken every 5 years. For prices and details see *Bureau of the Census Catalog*.

Cleveland Trust Company Business Bulletin. Monthly. Cleveland Trust Co., Euclid & East 9th Street, Cleveland, Ohio 44101. Current economic comments.

Commercial and Financial Chronicle. Semiweekly. Wm. B. Dana Company, 65 Park Place, New York, New York 10008. General corporate and investment news. The Monday issue includes a statistical section, the Thursday issue, general news.

The Conference Board Record. Monthly. National Industrial Conference Board, 845 Third Avenue, New York, New York 10022. Articles of interest to business economists and managers; reports on capital appropriations.

Construction Contracts. Monthly. F. W. Dodge Company, Division of McGraw-Hill Information Systems, 330 West 42nd Street, New York, New York 10036. Overall data are available in *Survey of Current Business*.

Construction Review. Monthly. U.S. Department of Commerce, GPO. Statistical tables on expenditures, building starts, materials, costs, awards, permits, employment; some interpretive text.

Construction Statistics, 1915–1964. U.S. Department of Commerce, GPO. Historical data for this series are shown in *Construction Review*.

Consumer Buying Prospects. Quarterly. Commercial Credit Company, 300 St. Paul Place, Baltimore, Maryland 21202. Processes raw data collected by the Bureau of the Census on consumer buying indicators to develop expected total consumer demand in units and in dollar totals.

Consumer Price Index. Monthly. U.S. Department of Labor, Bureau of Labor Statistics, Washington, D.C. 20212. Detailed information on components of the consumer price index.

Current Construction Reports. U.S. Department of Commerce, GPO. Reports on various aspects of public and private construction expenditures, housing starts, and permits.

Series C-20   Housing Starts. Monthly.
Series C-25   Sales of New One-Family Homes. Monthly, plus quarterly and annual supplements.
Series C-30   Value of New Construction Put in Place. Monthly, plus annual supplement.
Series C-40   New Housing Units Authorized by Local Building Permits. Monthly, plus annual supplement.

Current Foreign Trade Reports. Monthly. U.S. Department of Commerce, Bureau of the Census, Washington, D.C. 20233. Reports on exports and imports of merchandise trade and shipping and foreign airborne trade. Subscription includes:

Series FT 900   Export and Import Merchandise Trade.
Series FT 975   Vessel Entrances and Clearances.
Series FT 985   U.S. Waterborne Foreign Trade.
Series FT 986   U.S. Airborne Trade Customs District by Continent.

Current Housing Reports. U.S. Department of Commerce, GPO. Reports on housing vacancies and characteristics of housing units.

Series H-111   Housing Vacancies. Quarterly.
Series H-121   Housing Characteristics. Occasionally.

Current Industrial Reports: Manufacturers' Shipments, Inventories and Orders. Monthly. U.S. Department of Commerce, Bureau of the Census, Washington, D.C. 20233. Data on manufacturers' sales, inventories, new and unfilled orders, with detail by industries.

Current Population Reports. Irregularly. U.S. Department of Commerce, GPO. Monthly and special releases of data obtained from the U.S. Bureau of the Census' current population survey. Price includes:

Series P-20	Population Characteristics.
Series P-23	Technical Studies.
Series P-25	Population Estimates.
Series P-27	Farm Population.
Series P-28	Special Censuses.
Series P-60	Consumer Income.
Series P-65	Consumer Buying Indicators. Reports on recent purchases of automobiles and household durable goods by households and expected purchases during the months ahead.

Current Retail Trade Reports. U.S. Department of Commerce, GPO. Single subscription includes:

Weekly Retail Sales Report
Advance Monthly Retail Sales Report
Monthly Retail Trade Report
Annual Retail Trade Report

Current Selected Service Reports: Monthly Selected Service Receipts. Monthly. U.S. Department of Commerce, Bureau of the Census, Washington, D.C. 20233. Reports summary statistics on such services as hotels, motels, laundries, dry cleaning, beauty and barber shops, selected business services, miscellaneous repair services, motion pictures, and amusement and recreation services.

Daily Index Numbers and Spot Primary Market Prices. Weekly. U.S. Department of Labor, Bureau of Labor Statistics, Washington, D.C. 20250. Weekly summary issued each Wednesday showing daily indexes and prices through Tuesday.

Daily Statement of the United States Treasury. Daily. U.S. Department of the Treasury, GPO. Shows cash deposits and withdrawals. End of month statement includes detailed Statement of Public Debt.

Defense Indicators. Monthly. U.S. Department of Commerce, GPO. Brings together series on defense activity that influence short-term changes in the national economy. Includes series on obligations, contracts, orders, shipments, inventories, expenditures, employment, and earnings.

DMS Inc., a subsidiary of McGraw-Hill Publications. 100 Northfield Street, Greenwich, Connecticut 06830. Provides frequent market intelligence reports on federal defense, space, and electronics programs and on such civilian programs as air pollution. Also does forecasting of defense and, particularly, military and civilian aircraft production.

Dun's Review. Monthly. Dun & Bradstreet, Inc., P.O. Box 3088, Grand Central Station, New York, New York 10017. Contains statistical data on business failures.

Economic Indicators. Monthly. Prepared for the Joint Committee on the Economic Report by the Council of Economic Advisers, GPO. Data on total output, income and spending, employment, production prices, credit and federal finance. Presents gross national product quarterly estimates, which are made about three weeks after the end of the quarter.

> *Economic Indicators, Historical and Descriptive Supplements.* Latest edition, 1967. Describes each series published in *Economic Indicators* and gives data for years not shown in monthly issues.

Economic Report of the President, together with *The Annual Report by the Council of Economic Advisers.* Annually (before July 1952, semiannually). GPO. An important summary and discussion of the President's economic policies for the forthcoming year. Also contains a valuable statistical appendix.

Electric Power Output. Weekly. Edison Electric Institute, 750 Third Avenue, New York, New York 10017. Shows electrical energy distributed by electric light and power industry.

Employment and Earnings and Monthly Report of the Labor Force.

Monthly. U.S. Department of Labor, Bureau of Labor Statistics, GPO. Statistical material including labor force, employment and unemployment, payroll, employment by industry, hours and earnings, labor turnover. Releases available.

Engineering News-Record. Weekly. McGraw-Hill Publishing Company, Inc., 330 West 42nd Street, New York, New York 10036. Particular emphasis on construction and building news. Data on ENR contracts awarded and indexes of construction costs.

Expenditure Patterns of the American Family. Prepared by National Industrial Conference Board and sponsored by *Life.* New York: National Industrial Conference Board, 845 Third Avenue, New York 10022, 1965. Based on U.S. Department of Labor, *Survey of Consumer Expenditures, 1960–1961,* it provides a statistical profile of how the U.S. consumer lives. Contains average household expenditures for some 700 individual products and services according to selected family characteristics such as income, age, and occupation. (See also *Market Profiles of Consumer Products.*)

Federal Reserve Bank Monthly Reviews. Monthly.

Business Conditions. Federal Reserve Bank of Chicago, Box 834, Chicago, Illinois 60690.

Business Review. Federal Reserve Bank of Philadelphia, Philadelphia, Pennsylvania 19101.

Business Review. Federal Reserve Bank of Dallas, Dallas, Texas 75222.

Economic Review. Federal Reserve Bank of Cleveland, P.O. Box 6387, Cleveland, Ohio 44101.

Monthly Review. Federal Reserve Bank of San Francisco, 400 Sansome Street, San Francisco, California 94120.

Monthly Review. Federal Reserve Bank of Atlanta, Atlanta, Georgia 30303.

Monthly Review. Federal Reserve Bank of Kansas City, Federal Reserve Station, Kansas City, Missouri 64198.

Monthly Review. Federal Reserve Bank of New York, 33 Liberty Street, New York, New York. 10045.

Monthly Review. Federal Reserve Bank of Richmond, Richmond, Virginia 23213.

Monthly Statistical Report. Federal Reserve Bank of Minneapolis, Minneapolis, Minnesota 55440. Ninth District Conditions.

New England Business Review. Federal Reserve Bank of Boston, Boston, Massachusetts 02110.

Review. Federal Reserve Bank of St. Louis, St. Louis, Missouri 63102.

Also available:
Federal Budget Trends. Quarterly.
Monetary Trends. Monthly.
National Economic Trends. Monthly.
Rates of Change in Bank Reserves and Money. Monthly.
Triangles of U.S. Economic Data. Quarterly.
U.S. Balance of Payments Trends. Quarterly.
U.S. Financial Data. Weekly.

Federal Reserve Bulletin. Monthly. Board of Governors of the Federal Reserve System, Division of Administrative Services, Washington, D.C. 20551. Interpretive text and U.S. financial, industrial, and commercial statistics; international financial statistics. Mimeographed releases on many of the statistics regularly reported in the *Federal Reserve Bulletin* are available separately. Some of the more widely used are listed below:

Series E.5	Capacity Utilization in Manufacturing. Quarterly.
Series G.12.3	Business Indexes. Monthly.
Series G.18	Consumer Instalment Credit at Commercial Banks. Monthly.
Series G.19	Consumer Credit. Monthly.
Series G.20	Sales Finance Companies. Monthly.
Series G.26	Automobile Instalment Credit Developments. Monthly.
Series H.4.2	Weekly Condition Report of Large Commercial Banks. Weekly.

Series H.12   Commercial and Industrial Loans Outstanding by Industry. Weekly.

Series H.6   Monthly Supply and Time Deposits. Weekly.

Historical data for the Index of Industrial Production are available in *Industrial Production, 1957–1959 Base.*

Federal Reserve Chart Book. Monthly. Board of Governors of the Federal Reserve System, Washington, D.C. 20551. Plus the latest edition of *Historical Chart Book.*

First National City Bank Monthly Economic Letter: General Business Conditions. Monthly. First National City Bank of New York, 399 Park Avenue, New York, New York 10022. Comments on current economic conditions.

Flow of Funds Accounts, 1945–1967. Flow of Funds Section, Division of Research and Statistics, Board of Governors of the Federal Reserve System, Washington, D.C. 20551. Statistical data and explanation of accounts.

Fortune. Monthly (except two issues in May and August). Time, Inc., 540 North Michigan Avenue, Chicago, Illinois 60611. Articles of business interest. The monthly column Business Roundup includes results of *Fortune* surveys on business expectations.

Freight Car Loadings. Weekly. Association of American Railroads, 2 Penn Plaza, New York, New York 10001.

Governmental Finances. Annually. U.S. Department of Commerce, GPO. Contains data on state and local finances.

The Guaranty Survey. Monthly. Guaranty Trust Company of New York, P.O. Box 495, Church Street Station, New York, New York 10013. Interpretive text on domestic and foreign situation. Contains chart of Wholesale Price Index of Guaranty Trust Co. from 1919 to date (1926 = 100).

Handbook of Labor Statistics. Annually. U.S. Department of Labor, Bureau of Labor Statistics, GPO. Historical data on manpower, compensation, productivity, prices, industrial relations, and foreign labor statistics.

Housing Construction Statistics, 1889–1964. Washington, D.C.: U.S. Department of Commerce, GPO. Historical supplement to current data on housing starts and building permits. (See *Current Housing Reports.*)

Journal of Commerce. Daily except Saturdays, Sundays, and holidays. 99 Wall Street, New York, New York 10005. Particular emphasis on foreign trade, shipping, and commodities.

McGraw-Hill Information Systems Company. 330 West 42nd Street, New York, New York 10036.
> *Dodge Reports*
> *Dodge Construction Statistics*
> *Dodge Building Cost and Specification Digest*

Manufacturers Hanover Trust—Economic Report. Monthly. Manufacturers Hanover Trust, 350 Park Avenue, New York, New York 10022. Current economic comments.

Manufacturing Corporations—Quarterly Financial Report. Quarterly. Federal Trade Commission–Securities and Exchange Commission, GPO. Current profit and loss and balance sheet data for all U.S. manufacturing industries from 1947 to date.

Market Profiles of Consumer Products. Prepared by National Industrial Conference Board and sponsored by *Life.* New York: National Industrial Conference Board, 845 Third Avenue, New York 10022, 1967. This study is a companion to *Expenditure Patterns of the American Family.* It shows the proportion of total consumer buying accounted for by the various economic and social segments of the nation's households.

Monthly Labor Review. Monthly. U.S. Department of Labor, Bureau of Labor Statistics, GPO. Special articles in the fields of labor relations, labor economics, and labor statistics. Statistics on labor force employment, labor turnover, earnings, hours, consumer and

wholesale prices, work stoppages, and productivity. Separate proc-
essed reports present more detailed and additional data on subjects covered in the *Monthly Labor Review*. (See *Handbook of
Labor Statistics*.)

Monthly Retail Trade Report. Monthly. U.S. Department of Commerce, GPO. Data on sales and inventories by industries, geographic regions, and selected standard metropolitan areas. (See
Current Retail Trade Reports.)

Monthly Review. Monthly. New York Stock Exchange, 11 Wall
Street, New York, New York 10005. Contains summary data on
transactions on the New York Stock Exchange, including the New
York Stock Exchange stock price indexes.

Monthly Statement of Budget Receipts & Expenditures. Monthly.
U.S. Department of the Treasury, GPO. Detailed budget receipts
and expenditures. (See *Daily Statement of the United States
Treasury*.)

Monthly Vital Statistics Report. Monthly. U.S. Department of
Health, Education and Welfare, Public Health Service, National
Office of Vital Statistics, 330 Independence Avenue, S.W., Washington, D.C. 20201. Contains provisional statistics on births, marriages, deaths, and divorces.

Monthly Wholesale Trade Report. Monthly. U.S. Department of
Commerce, Bureau of the Census, GPO. Data on sales and inventories by industries and geographic regions.

Moody's Stock Survey and Moody's Bond Survey. Weekly. Moody's
Investors Services, 99 Church Street, New York, New York 10003.
Current weekly data on stock and bond yields.

Motor Vehicles (cars and trucks assembled). Weekly. Ward's Reports,
Inc., 550 West Fort Street, Detroit, Michigan 48226. Total pas-
senger car and truck output in the United States.

National Economic Projections. Annually. National Planning Association, 1606 New Hampshire Avenue, N.W., Washington, D.C. 20009. Detailed projections for major sectors of the economy for five and ten years ahead. Plus technical analysis of various forecasting problems.

New Business Incorporations. Monthly. Dun & Bradstreet, Inc., P.O. Box 803, New York, New York 10008. Number of businesses incorporated by states, comparisons for previous periods, and analysis of data.

New York Times. Daily. 229 West 43rd Street, New York, New York 10036. General economic information and news. Contains data on *The New York Times* stock price index.

Newsweek. Weekly. Newsweek, Inc., 350 Dennison Avenue, Dayton, Ohio 45401. Includes capital appropriations studies prepared by the National Industrial Conference Board.

Paperboard Production. Weekly. American Paper Institute, 260 Madison Avenue, New York, New York 10016.

Pick's Currency Yearbook. Annually. Pick Publishing Corporation, New York, New York 10006. Contains information on unofficial as well as official exchange rates.

Population—Census. Decennially. U.S. Department of Commerce, Bureau of the Census, GPO. Complete enumeration of population taken every ten years since 1790. Eighteenth census taken in 1960.

Population Index. Quarterly. Office of Population Research, Princeton University, Princeton, New Jersey 08540. Contains extensive international bibliography.

Reports of Consultant Committees. Organized by Board of Governors of the Federal Reserve System at the request of the Subcommittee on Economic Statistics of the Joint Committee on the Economic Report. Federal Reserve Board, Washington, D.C. 20551.

Report of the Consultant Committee on Savings Statistics. July 1955.

Report of the Consultant Committee on Plant and Equipment Expenditure Expectations. July 1955.

Report of the Consultant Committee on Consumer Expectations. July 1955.

Report of the Consultant Committee on General Business Expectations. September 1955.

Report of the Consultant Committee on Inventory Statistics. November 1955.

Social Security Bulletin. Monthly. U.S. Department of Health, Education and Welfare, Social Security Administration, GPO. Interpretive text and statistical data on social security programs. Annual statistical and historical data published in the Supplements.

Standard & Poor's Current Statistics. Monthly. Standard & Poor's Corporation, 345 Hudson Street, New York, New York 10014. Contains, among other things, data on Standard & Poor's stock indexes and quarterly earnings, dividends, and price earnings ratio based on Standard & Poor's daily stock price indexes. Historical data given in *Security Price Index Record*, published annually.

Standard & Poor's Outlook. Weekly. Contains weekly data on bond and stock yields.

Statistical Abstract of the United States. Annually. U.S. Department of Commerce, Bureau of the Census, GPO. Important summary statistics obtained from government and nongovernment sources. Also contains a bibliography of sources of statistical data. Plus *Supplements.*

Historical Statistics of the United States, Colonial Times to 1957. Washington, D.C. GPO, 1960. Presents about 3,000 statistical time series, largely annual, extending back to the earliest year for which data are available with sources, notes, and descriptions.

Historical Statistics of the United States, Colonial Times to 1957. Washington, D.C.: GPO, 1965. Continuation to 1962 and revisions.

Statistical Bulletin. Monthly. Metropolitan Life Insurance Company, 1 Madison Avenue, New York, New York 10010. Articles of current interest on population.

Statistical Bulletin. Monthly. U.S. Securities and Exchange Commission, GPO. Statistical tables on securities offerings, exchange, assets and liabilities of corporations, individual savings, plant and equipment expenditures. Releases available.

Statistical Indicator. Weekly. Statistical Indicator Associates, North Egremont, Massachusetts 01252. Provides current data on statistical indicators of the National Bureau of Economic Research.

Statistical Reporter. Monthly. U.S. Bureau of the Budget, Office of Statistical Standards, GPO. Prepared primarily for the interchange of information among government employees engaged in statistical research activities. Comments on new government reports and programs.

Statistical Services of the U.S. Government. Irregularly. U.S. Bureau of the Budget, Office of Statistical Standards, GPO. Designed to serve as a basic reference document on the statistical programs of the U.S. government.

Statistics of Income. Annually. U.S. Department of the Treasury, GPO. Tax, income, and related data compiled from income tax returns. Separate reports on Individuals, Corporations, All Business, and Fiduciary, Gift and Estate.

Steel Production. Weekly. American Iron & Steel Institute, 150 East 42nd Street, New York, New York 10017. Production of steel ingots and steel for castings.

Survey of Consumer Expenditures, 1960–1961. U.S. Department of Labor, Bureau of Labor Statistics, Washington, D.C. 20212. The BLS has issued almost 200 reports summarizing the results of its survey of consumer expenditures in 1960–1961. This is an invaluable source of material for anyone studying consumption patterns. Average expenditures for major components of family expenditures are reported by family income (after taxes), family size, age of head, occupation of head, education of head, color market location, and so on. In addition, some cross classification of characteristics is shown. For selected family characteristics, expenditures are also given in considerable detail.

Survey of Consumer Finances. Annually. Survey Research Center, Institute for Social Research, The University of Michigan, Ann Arbor, Michigan 48104. Since 1960, the Survey Research Center has published in these volumes its survey data on consumer finances, attitudes, and inclinations to buy.

Survey of Current Business. Monthly, including weekly statistical supplement. U.S. Department of Commerce, Office of Business Economics, GPO. Interpretive text and charts of current business trends; includes about 2,500 statistical series. Contains quarterly estimates. The *Survey of Current Business* annual February issue provides preliminary estimates for the preceding year. The annual July issue provides revised data covering three latest years for all series presented in the National Income and Gross National Product supplement. News releases are also available. These reports are regular releases that are issued prior to their publication in the *Survey of Current Business*. Some of the more important ones are listed below.

Balance of International Payments. Quarterly.

Manufacturers' Inventories and Sales Expectations. Quarterly.

National Income and Gross National Product. Quarterly. Gives preliminary quarterly data about six weeks after the end of the quarter. Data on corporate profits and national income are not available until about fifteen weeks after the end of the quarter.

Personal Income. Monthly.

Plant & Equipment Expenditures of United States Business. Quarterly.

Manufacturing and Trade Inventories and Sales. Monthly.

Wholesalers' Sales & Inventories. Monthly.

Business Statistics. Biennially; latest edition 1967. Basic handbook giving past data on series shown monthly in *Survey of Current Business*.

National Income Supplements. Irregularly. The latest issue is *The National Income and Product Accounts of the United States, 1929–1965.* Other supplements include *U.S. Income and Output, A Supplement to the Survey of Current Business,* 1958, and *National Income, A Supplement to the Survey of Current Business,* 1954.

Treasury Bulletin. Monthly. U.S. Department of the Treasury, GPO. Statistical tables on all phases of federal government fiscal operations.

Unemployment Insurance Claims. Weekly. U.S. Department of Labor, Manpower Administration, 14th Street and Constitution Avenue, Washington, D.C. 20210. Provides data on initial claims and insured unemployment under state unemployment insurance; unemployment compensation for veterans and for federal employees programs.

Unemployment Insurance Review. Monthly. U.S. Department of Labor, Manpower Administration, 14th Street and Constitution Avenue, Washington, D.C. 20210.

Unemployment Insurance Statistics. Monthly. U.S. Department of Labor, Manpower Administration, 14th Street and Constitution Avenue, Washington, D.C. 20210.

The U.S. Industrial Outlook. Annually. U.S. Department of Commerce, GPO. Contains outlook statements for key manufacturing industries. Includes data on production, sales, employment productivity, and so on.

Vital Statistics—Special Reports—National Summaries. Irregularly. U.S. Department of Health, Education and Welfare, National Office of Vital Statistics, 330 Independence Avenue, S.W., Washington, D.C. 20210. Final and detailed statistics on births, marriages, deaths, and divorces.

   Vital Statistics—Special Reports—Selected Studies. Irregularly. Analysis of vital statistics.

Wall Street Journal. Daily except Saturdays, Sundays, and holidays. 200 Burnett Road, Chicopee, Massachusetts 01021. Particular emphasis on articles of investment significance. Statistical information on Dow Jones stock price averages.

Weekly Retail Sales Report. Weekly. U.S. Department of Commerce, GPO. (See *Current Retail Trade Reports.*)

Wholesale Commodity Prices. Weekly. Dun & Bradstreet, Inc., P.O. Box 803, New York, New York 10008. Price changes in thirty basic commodities and in Dun & Bradstreet's daily sensitive spot index, with comments. Issued Tuesdays.

Wholesale (Primary Market) Price Index and Economic Sector Index. Monthly. U.S. Department of Labor, Bureau of Labor Statistics, Washington, D.C. 20212. Prices for individual commodities, groups, subgroups, and product classes, and price relatives for individual commodities.

INDEX

The Authors

LEONARD S. SILK is a Senior Fellow at the Brookings Institution, Washington, D.C. He was formerly Editorial Page Editor and Chairman of the Board of Editors of *Business Week*. In 1965–1966 he was Ford Foundation Distinguished Visiting Research Professor at Carnegie-Mellon University. In 1967 he served as a member of the President's Commission on Budget Concepts. He is a Fellow of the National Association of Business Economists and a member of the American Economic Association and the American Association for the Advancement of Science. He received his Ph.D. in economics from Duke University.

M. LOUISE CURLEY is Vice President, Economics with Scudder, Stevens & Clark, one of the oldest and largest investment counsel partnerships. She is a member of the American Economic Association, the American Statistical Association, the Econometric Society, and the Population Association. She received her Ph.D. in economics from the Massachusetts Institute of Technology.